STARS SEEN IN PERSON

T0151280

STARS SEEN IN PERSON

Selected Journals

JOHN WIENERS

Edited with an Introduction by Michael Seth Stewart
Preface by Ammiel Alcalay

 City Lights Books | San Francisco

Library of Congress Cataloging-in-Publication Data

Wieners, John, 1934-2002.
 [Works. Selections]
 Stars seen in person : selected journals of John Wieners / edited by
Michael Seth Stewart ; preface by Ammiel Alcalay.
     pages cm
 ISBN 978-0-87286-668-3 (paperback)
 1. Wieners, John, 1934-2002. 2. Poets, American—20th century—
Biography. I. Stewart, Michael Seth, editor. II. Alcalay, Ammiel, writer
of preface. III. Title.
 PS3573.I35A6 2015
 818'.5403—dc23
 [B]
                              2015023040

City Lights Books are published at the City Lights Bookstore
261 Columbus Avenue, San Francisco, CA 94133
www.citylights.com

Contents

Preface

Ammiel Alcalay

In Friendship
"Why is it a major poet seems impossible
to write about, while the ingratiating success yields
odes of dazzling elegy & national award"
—John Wieners, in "The Cut (*After Reading Gerard
Malanga's Interview with Charles Olson* in The Paris
Review, *Summer 1970*)"

I learned about the death of John Wieners in 2002 through
a phone call from poet and old friend Duncan McNaughton.
He had died on my birthday and I was attending an academic
conference, very rare for me, on the partition of India, Ireland,
and Palestine. I had gone mainly to be with old friends who
seldom had a chance to gather. But after speaking to Duncan, I
realized there was no one there I could share the news with, or
at least no one who would immediately grasp the significance
of the loss. The details came later, from John's stalwart friend
Jim Dunn, about how John had left a party and collapsed on
his way home, found by a parking lot attendant and taken to
the hospital. Not having any ID on him, it was only through
the persistence of a social worker and some nurses that he was
identified at all. This scenario almost played out John's answer
to scholar Robert van Hallberg's 1974 question, posed in a
rare interview: "For whom do you write?" he asked. "For the
poetical, the people." Wieners responded, "Not for myself,
merely. Or ever. Only for the better, warm, human loving, kind
person. The guy on the street who might hold open a door for

you . . . stops to give you instructions, spares some change, lets you in his bookshop. Friends I take for granted, like the future."

My encounter with John Wieners was early, and personal. That is, I met him as a teenager while hanging out either at then Gordon Cairnie's Grolier Books or the Temple Bar Bookshop, run by Jim and Gene, the O'Neil brothers, both in Cambridge. Cambridge MASS, with an emphasis on the long broad "A" that the rest of the country once might have been familiar with through President John F. Kennedy. Since then it's only been an occasional movie or, among poets, the singular voice of Eileen Myles. That's part of a bigger story, in which the Boston John Wieners came from and mainly lived in was/is an actual place, peopled by a particular accent that, in John's case, was immediately recognizable, almost archaic.

This first encounter would have most likely taken place sometime in 1969. I had just become a teenager and was drawn to everything *outside* of school: playing hockey at the Commons; taking in triple features at the Stuart in the combat zone while ducking the truant officer; shooting pool from one end of town to the other; going up the fire escapes to sneak into the Boston Garden with friends from the North End; sitting in the right field grandstands at Fenway for less than two bucks; listening to young men, not that much older than me, seeking asylum from the draft at the Arlington Street Church; talking to kids from Roxbury selling the Black Panther Party paper which I bought religiously every week and read from cover to cover; gravitating from bookstores to demonstrations and back again, depending on what might be happening in the streets of our world.

I often found myself in what might have seemed strange circumstances, but I never questioned them. All the while I raided my parents' bookshelves, loaded with little magazines of the 1950s and 60s: *Black Mountain Review*, *Big Table*, *Evergreen*, *Yugen*, and so many others, never thinking it unusual. When Jack Kerouac died in October 1969, I was irate, knowing he'd been forgotten, and viscerally feeling that he'd somehow been assassinated by society. I knew that most of his books were out of print because you couldn't find the ones we had at home in bookstores. I asked family friend Vincent Ferrini, the Gloucester poet to whom Charles Olson's *Maximus Poems* were first addressed as a series of letters, what to do. He suggested I write to Allen Ginsberg, which I did. I then suddenly found a use for school and proceeded to write a militant twenty-five page typed single spaced paper in which I went on the offensive, reviewing Kerouac's work for a teacher I was sure would be uninterested or taken aback by my attitude, and I poured it on, making damn sure that would be the case.

Not long after Kerouac's death came the news of Charles Olson, another family friend, going into hospital in New York. Through a conversation at one of the bookstores, I was given to understand that a book dealer had appeared with a stack of books for Olson to sign. Outraged, I wrote a near libelous letter to the dealer who was ready to sue me until he heard how old I was. Throughout, John was a presence. I would see him at the Grolier and we'd walk to the Temple Bar, or the other way around. Sometimes I'd sit with him at the Hayes-Bickford's in Harvard Square. Other times I found myself at gatherings with a group of older people, not knowing exactly what they might be going through, but never feeling unwanted or uncomfortable. Along the way he'd give me books or broadsides, always signed to me: *Ace of Pentacles*, *Asylum Poems*, *The Hotel Wentley Poems*, *Nerves*, *Pressed Wafer*, *A Letter to Charles Olson*. Once he gave me an old copy of *Amiel's Journal*, by the Swiss philosopher-poet Henri Amiel, published in the 1880s. When my mother and I went to Olson's funeral in Gloucester, John was there, among the pallbearers, who included Ferrini, Peter Anastas (another old Gloucester friend), legendary patron of the arts and Frontier Press publisher Harvey Brown, scholar and translator Charles Boer, poets Ed Dorn, Allen Ginsberg, and Ed Sanders.

Back in Boston, there was a visit to poet Steve Jonas's apartment, somewhere near the Charles Street Jail, on the other side of Beacon Hill, in the palpably absent shadow of John's beloved Scollay Square, victim of the juggernaut wrecking ball of "urban renewal." There was a reading at the Charles Street Meeting House where I took pictures, as I often did then, with black and white film that I developed and printed, some of them gracing the walls of the Grolier or given to the poets when I had the chance. From that night there were pictures of John along with Denise Levertov, Anne Sexton, and Ron Loewinsohn. I always thought the reading must have been for some political cause but everyone I asked in Boston over the years couldn't remember or said no such event took place. It was only in 2012, while working on a *Lost & Found* project with poet Joanne Kyger, that she sent me the copy of a letter from John to her, dated February 22, 1970, in which he wrote: "Monday evening I gave a benefit for the Chicago 7 at the Charles Street Meeting House with Denise Levertov, Anne Sexton, Ron Loewinsohn, James Tate, etc." Jonas had died just twelve days before John's letter was written. I remember the shock wave that both Olson and Jonas's deaths had sent through this familial group of older poets that I found myself in the company of. I'm not sure what exactly I understood, but I knew that these events, like so many of the things we were demonstrating about, were momentous.

The intricacies of this particular history, what poet Gerrit Lansing has called "the occult school of Boston" (as mentioned by Seth Stewart in his introduction), is one of the many chapters of North American cultural and political life from the second half of the 20th century yet to be fully documented or even remotely understood by those who weren't, in at least some way, part of them. While celebrated throughout his lifetime as a unique and masterful lyric poet by the most important poets of the period, the availability of Wieners's work has varied wildly. Receiving no critical acknowledgement or recognition during and even after his lifetime, gathering the work has mainly been the task of dedicated friends.

When most of his early small press books had become increasingly hard to find, Raymond Foye edited two superb volumes for Black Sparrow Press, *Selected Poems 1958-1984* (1986), and *Cultural Affairs in Boston: Poetry & Prose 1956-1985* (1988), gathering previous collections and uncollected works, as well as the few extant interviews that Wieners had given (with Foye, Charlie Shively, and Robert van Hallberg). The introductions to those books, by Allen Ginsberg and Robert Creeley, provided, for the time, the clearest responses and assessments of his work. William Corbett, at some point, published a facsimile edition of *The Hotel Wentley Poems*, feeling the need for people to read something akin to the original version of that landmark book, published by the late Dave Haselwood as the first title of Auerhahn Press in 1958. Over the years, many people have sheltered, gathered, pirated, written about, and published the work of John Wieners, and a complete list would become a who's who of the poetry world of the past six decades.

With the publication of these journals, through Seth Stewart's erudite and meticulous editorship, the possibility of beginning to see Wieners' work in its fullness comes that much closer to realization. Parallel to the journals, a new *Selected Works* (edited by Joshua Beckman, CAConrad, and Robert Dewhurst) has come out. In addition, Stewart has completed an extraordinary critical edition of Wieners' collected correspondence, covering important exchanges between Wieners and Olson, Robert Duncan, Robert Creeley, Denise Levertov, Michael Rumaker, Edward Dorn, Diane di Prima, Amiri Baraka, Philip Whalen, Joanne Kyger, and many others. Parallel to the correspondence, Dewhurst has been preparing a *Collected Poems*. As Stewart has put it, "I consider these projects together as a *habeas corpus* mission, an effort to "produce the body" of Wieners' thought, works, and life, liberating him from the institutions that subsumed him, that "official verse culture" that could not accommodate a poor, homosexual, visionary poet who refused to be simply one of those things."

II.

In a 1972 text, Wieners wrote: "Since 1955, poetry or verse as some would prefer it be called has, despite all forebodings that it was dying, taken through a handful of writers in the United States, a stranglehold on established modes of thought, analysis, and attention." Marking this at 1955 meant, for Wieners, recognition of a now very obscure but enormously influential poem, Ed Marshall's "Leave the Word Alone," included in Donald M. Allen's landmark 1960 anthology *The New American Poetry*. He goes on to mention, among others, Charlie Parker, a figure that looms large for the poets of the period. Jack Kerouac delineated Parker's significance very particularly when he talked of bop as "the language of America's inevitable Africa," but an idiom "no one understands because the language isn't alive in the land yet." Making such a language live—a language arrived at in relation to the world, as a statement about the kind of world that had come into being— is certainly a strand running throughout the artistic stance of the period, in every medium, and part of the "stranglehold on established modes of thought, analysis, and attention" that Wieners refers to.

We should never lose sight of the fact that this great period of cultural activity—by artists in various forms and media: musicians, painters, dancers, poets— took place at the height of the Cold War, and in a place of isolation so acute that, as Gary Snyder once remarked, "you'd hitchhike 1500 miles to see a friend." As the administration of knowledge grew with the expansion of universities and the military/industrial complex, artists struggled to redefine the parameters of knowledge, but completely outside the framework of official institutions and structures. Without enough money for long distance phone calls or frequent travel, the most vital records of thought in the United States following World War II took place in conversation, private journals or through correspondence, in letters, a venue still fairly well protected from the reach of surveillance.

Our adulation of the individual, tied to the destruction of any collectivity or commons, dictates that our cultural figures remain lonely, unmoored from friends, lovers, competitors, idols or places of reference, unless some scandal or possibility of ideological hijacking might be involved. From our present vantage point, it takes more than some mental gymnastics to grasp the excitement, for example, of Jack Kerouac when he writes in a 1957 letter to Allen Ginsberg about how excited he is that John Wieners, newly arrived to San Francisco following the dissolution of Black Mountain College, wants to publish a few of his poems in a new magazine Wieners has launched called *Measure*. Or that the late Amiri Baraka, then LeRoi Jones, became John's legal guardian after a hospitalization. Needless to say, most readers will never have heard of this incident or *Measure*, a magazine lasting three issues over a span of five years, but with the greater availability of Wieners' work—particularly the journals and letters—his absence in the historical record can start to be addressed. Ironically, while Wieners remained largely obscure in his lifetime, he was beloved by other poets and his survival depended on friendships, while Kerouac was turned into product, eaten alive by the relentless machinery of consumption. The return to materials that have been withdrawn, the creation of a world of beauty out of them, is a turn to what Olson called "the gold machine," interpreted by scholar Miriam Nichols as "an alchemical trope that makes actual things rise up as concretely *in situ* as possible, thus to trouble generic representations—to throw the disturbance of actuality into the universe of discourse." This troubling of generic representation is also, in this case, the multiply complex individual—John Wieners—that, as Seth Stewart emphasizes, could not be accommodated by either "official verse culture" or "the universe of discourse." The universe that John dwelt in was filled with harsh reality—forced electroshock and insulin therapy, poverty, addiction, despair—but out of it he forged a world of truth and beauty. His absolute mastery of form should, by all critical criteria, have put to shame all of his conventional prize-winning and celebrated contemporaries purportedly working in traditional forms. But such a thing could not be for it would signal an admittance of reality and historical consciousness into a world of propaganda, disinformation, and absolute counter-factual fabrication. In the face of a systemic violence that attempts to destroy any lasting record of the contradictory real, relegating the very material of our most intimate history to oblivion, I have no doubt that John's work will remain as an act of singular courage and testimony to the lives we actually lived.

Ammiel Alcalay
January 22, 2015

Introduction
Michael Seth Stewart

When asked what school of poetry he belonged to, John Wieners identified as "a Boston poet." He doesn't so much document Boston as embody it, giving it syllable and line to echo its speech, its gentility and subterranean pleasures. He is writing from a Boston that no longer exists, that got plowed over for the brutal urban renewal of the nineteen sixties, the Boston of Scollay Square and dive bars one could afford, of burlesque queens and movie houses where one could stare at the stars. Except for a fifteen-year stretch, John Wieners lived all his life in Boston or one of its suburbs. Those years contained all his lives in centers of poetry—Black Mountain, San Francisco, New York, and Buffalo—and the greatest share of his output. This was the span of time in which he wrote most of his crowning achievements—from *The Hotel Wentley Poems* in 1958 through 1969's *Asylum Poems*—books that show a mind on fire for his work, for the poem, "the song of life, soft syllables from God."

John Wieners grew up in working-class Milton, Massachusetts, just outside Boston. He was a child of the Depression, a member of the so-called Silent Generation, the one conscripted into service in Korea, too young for World War II and too old for Vietnam. He started Boston College at sixteen, knowing out of the gate that he was going to be a Poet, a vocation he knew, from his devoured poetry books and gossip magazines, would lead to heartache and possibly glory. At school, beneath the oppressive eyes of the Jesuits, he found safe havens with other nascent bohemians, budding poets and artists with whom he could gab in the offices of the student lit-mag and the bars and coffee shops of Beacon Hill, swooning over Edna St Vincent Millay and Zelda Fitzgerald, like many of their generation obsessed with the legendary flair and freedom of the nineteen twenties. The rest of the decade was marked by this lust for life, a Rimbaldian excessiveness that, by the end of 1959, so alarmed his family they had him committed, the first of several forced hospitalizations.

With the four books in this collection, Wieners' known journals are now all in print, seven fascinating books that vary wildly in style, intent, and relative coherence, altogether defying categorization. His first published journal, the only one released in his lifetime, was released in 1997 as *The Journal of John Wieners is to be called 707 Scott Street for Billie Holiday* (Sun & Moon Press). Written in San Francisco around the time of *The Hotel Wentley Poems*, the journal opened a window into Wieners' developing poetics and wide reading at the time, making it clear that *The Hotel Wentley* Poems was not the fluke product of some tripping prodigy, but the culmination of several years' work. "Last night I saw Greta Garbo one instant," he writes in 1959, before turning abruptly: "All I am interested in is charting the progress of my own soul. And therefore all men's souls. What the soul is I don't know."

In 2007, five years after Wieners' death, Bootstrap Press released another journal, *A Book of Prophecies*, a lyric, fragmented book written between 1970 and 1972. This was followed in 2010 by Bootstrap's ornate edition of *A New Book From Rome*, a red-and-gilt book of poems and fragments that Wieners wrote in the latter part of 1969, during another punishing six-month stretch in a state asylum. These later books explore many of the themes he writes about in the 1969 journal included here, in short lyric poems interspersed with lists and mini-essays on figures like Charles Olson and madness. This mix of memoir, poetry fragments, false starts, and lists—primarily of movies or celebrities he's seen—is perhaps the dominant mode of Wieners' journals, however varied they are in so many other ways. Always there is the work of poetry, and his memories and theories of that work, and a record of obsessions. Like the 1969 journal, which ends with a long list of "Stars Seen in Person," *Book of Prophecies* ends with "Seen or Encountered in Boston," "Poets I Have Met," and "Presents My Mother Gave Me," a charming two-year recollection including "room," "cigarettes," and "visits." And fittingly, the first of these books, *The Untitled Journal of a Would-Be Poet*, begins with recollections of his guiding star as a young poet, Edna St. Vincent Millay.

*

The journal swings between private and public like a door, oscillating—often within the same entry—between intensely personal address and an outward-facing stance which is confident in its eventual audience. There are different kinds of journals—the poet's book filled with scraps of verse and overheard phrases, the artist's sketchbook, the regular daybook lined with minutiae—and John Wieners' own journals run the gamut. Some, like 1955's *Untitled Journal of a Would-Be Poet*, are intensely self- and reader-conscious, the writing a discipline of preservation and refinement, passages crossed out and rewritten as he hones the best way of telling his story. By contrast, the 1966 journal is painfully naked, working through intense personal dramas by narrativizing and timelining the events of his life.

Somewhere midway on the spectrum are the dazzling journals—poets' books? —from 1959 and 1965, *707 Scott Street* and *Blaauwildebeestefontein*. Written while living with

Joanne Kyger and Wallace Berman, respectively, they were self-contained, thematically and aesthetically. The books are written during times of repose for the young poet, on Kyger's sofa in San Francisco and Berman's porch in Topanga Canyon, and contain reflections on poetics that distill Wieners' visions at those moments. *707 Scott Street* has long been an essential part of Wieners' canon, and *Blaauwildebeestefontein* stands alongside it, the meditations on process and life an expression of the six years of greatness and trauma lived between the two journals.

This is how we tell what kind of journal—or book—each one was meant to be, by studying it for clues. The self-contained 1959 and 1965 journals are decorated and very public in feel: for example, the 1965 journal includes a long section, rewritten in parts, explaining the history of Boston poetry. The 1955 journal, by contrast, is largely written according to a fixed daily quota, for a brief burst of time (picked back up a year later for just a couple of post-Black Mountain entries), with disciplined daily writing the goal. However, even among all its "I must write today, I must I must" type entries there are poems and lyric narrative sequences—in one case, rewritten twice more within the journal—that indicate a writing toward futurity. This is all, of course, in addition to the title: *The Untitled Journal of a Would-Be Poet*, intensely self-aware and self-deprecating, affecting a modesty that is belied by the book's assured, relatively sophisticated voice.

This first journal begins in the early winter months of 1955, just before his twenty-first birthday and just after his graduation from Boston College. He confesses in this "untitled journal" that he still loves Edna St. Vincent Millay, "despite her great faults," made ecstatic by the musicality of her light verse. Appropriately, the journal opens with a breezy recounting of this period, from across the gulf of graduation and, though it goes unmentioned in the journal till the end, his fateful encounter with Charles Olson at the Charles Street Meeting House. That performance would draw him to Olson's inspirations—notably Williams and Pound—and then down to North Carolina to study with the man himself, a relationship that endured the fifteen years till Olson's death. But for now, in January 1955, Olson is still in the background, as the young "would-be poet" studies Pound and works on his self-discipline, knowing the great work it will take to become what he considers a real poet, the vocation he would pursue with singular focus for the rest of his life.

But, of course, the young poet keeps getting distracted, keeps getting pulled into the world of the "golden people" with their "loud laughing" ("I love loud laughing," he writes), and he uses his journal to define himself against this cast of characters: Rita, a flirty friend he met at the art museum; the brainy Pat from Providence who "pants for life"; Robert Greene, his best friend from his Boston College literary magazine days; and a shadowy presence at first called "god" and finally identified as his first lover, a handsome blonde firefighter named Dana. At the same time, he's reading everyone Olson read, and the poets they cited as influences, excitedly noting his favorite lines and observations about the line and the breath, so influenced by Olson's 1950 essay "Projective Verse." The work culminates with his first semester at Black Mountain College, the summer of 1955, and there is a year's gap in the journal as he labored at his poetry and perpetually fraught relationship with Dana. Finally he revisits the book in September 1956 after his second term at the school, during a pause in his life as he decided whether to return to Black Mountain or stay in Boston and work out a life with Dana and the poets of Boston. He chose the latter, and in turn formed lifelong relationships with the influx of poets in 1956-57, writing and drinking with visitors Robin Blaser, Jack Spicer, and Frank O'Hara, and familiar faces Edward Marshall, Steve Jonas, and Joe and Carolyn Dunn, the libertines on Beacon Hill's working-class north slope, a pack that their friend Gerrit Lansing would aptly call "the occult school of Boston poetry," the group both occulted and driven by occult fascinations.

Appropriately, the journal ends with Wieners' desire to remain with Dana and "the most exciting part of love, the plan one makes to be loved, the traps one sets for love." By the fall of 1957, he and Dana would join many of their friends in migration to San Francisco, where he would continue in many unexpected ways the plan of study begun after the Charles Street Meeting House reading, as well as the social networking that went into his small magazine *Measure*. By the time he reached San Francisco, he was well established in the loose network of "New American Poets," and would produce during his stay there the two great monuments of his youth, *The Hotel Wentley Poems* and *707 Scott Street*.

His first hospitalization was in 1960, after a manic visit home frightened his parents into committing him for six months. His friends rallied to his side, petitioning doctors and lawyers, taking care of him upon release. He shuttled back and forth between his parents' home and the East Village of Manhattan, where he worked sometimes at the 8th Street Bookshop, wrote plays for the New York Poets' Theatre, and began his first full-length collection, 1964's *Ace of Pentacles*.

The second of these journals was written just after this strange time in late summer of 1965, a spectacular season for Wieners and for poetry. First he was able, through some maneuvering by Frank O'Hara, to accompany Olson to Spoleto, Italy, for the Festival of the Two Worlds. He met many literary lions but the pinnacle for him was meeting Ezra Pound, the gnarled poet celebrated (and protested) as a centerpiece of the festival. Like the other poets—a wide range, from Pound to John

Ashbery to Pier Paolo Pasolini—Wieners read in the ornate Cato Melisso. "What a ball," he described the trip in a letter to Wallace Berman. "I hope I can keep my cool." New York poet Bill Berkson also read at the festival, and while traveling picked up the leather journal for John Wieners that would, four years later, be filled and remembered as his *New Book From Rome*.

From Spoleto he went west for the Berkeley Poetry Conference, a twelve-day convocation, the kind of event that seemed legendary even as it happened. Wieners had his own night for reading, July 14. Olson's two events were epic performances, one a seminar on "Causal Mythology" and the other a rollicking, drunk poetry performance-slash-extemporaneous monologue on poetics and history, among other things. Wieners stayed with Joanne Kyger in San Francisco, making the trip together over to Berkeley every day for the seminars and readings. By August he was exhausted, and went to relax with old friend Wallace Berman, who lived with wife and son in Los Angeles, working on his magnificent small art magazine *Semina*. Staying there in the hills of Southern California, Wieners wrote a journal he called *Blaauwildebeestefontein*, in a bound black sketchbook featuring a pasted-on photo of naked Berman (with face scratched out, presumably out of discretion).

This journal brims with vital new poems, including drafts of an elegy written soon after Jack Spicer's premature death, but also some of his greatest explorations of poetics since *707 Scott Street*, such as an unparalleled history of his mid-nineteen-fifties poetry scene in Boston. His mission in this history is to place his friends, poets Edward Marshall and Steve Jonas, at the heart of not just Boston poetry, but the New American poetics across the board. He insists upon the primacy of Marshall's 1955 "Leave the Word Alone"—a scorching jeremiad whose passion and openness would inspire Allen Ginsberg in his composition of "Kaddish"—calling it "the first magnificent long poem of the century," written after "Steve Jonas first presented orders to us in the early years of the decade." His ruminations on Marshall and Steve Jonas are especially important contributions to the emergent histories of the New American Poets and the poets they loved, and the only time within Wieners' corpus of poems, journals, and letters in which he explicitly addresses their shared history and legacies.

The third and fourth journals in this collection come from the late 1960s, when Wieners was living in Buffalo, working on new poetry and studying again with Charles Olson. The university's new poetics program offered a teaching assistant's meager but steady paycheck and the chance to study with his teacher again, and so he moved there in January of 1965. Soon, however, Olson moved back to Gloucester, and the college town was stifling for Wieners, exacerbating an already fragile psychological state.

In 1966 he fell in love with a woman, well-known patron of the arts Panna Grady. She rented a house for the summer in Annisquam, up the road from Olson's Gloucester, and Wieners moved in. Living there with Grady and her daughter, Wieners flung himself with great gusto into the family-man role that decades of Catholicism had urged him towards. "Who would believe it?" he wrote in his journal, the third in this collection. "That the most notorious faggot of our times would fall in love with the best most beautiful woman." But the good times would not last long. As the relationship disintegrated, Grady became pregnant, and she chose to terminate the pregnancy. Wieners' reaction in his journal is difficult reading. But amidst the pained confession is the beginning of a new phase in his poetry, work that would continue in his books *Pressed Wafer, Asylum Poems,* and *Nerves,* which Allen Ginsberg would call "three magisterial books of poetry that stand among the few truthful monuments of the late 1960s era." The last of these three begins with "Supplication," an appeal to poetry to "give me a wife and home":

> Return me to the men who teach
> and above all, cure the
> hurts of wanting the impossible
> through this suspended vacuum.

Over the following two years, he became obsessed with old friend Robert Creeley, who Wieners was convinced was conspiring to harm him. "Unhappily his circumstances are very difficult," Creeley wrote to a mutual friend. "He is a brilliant poet, and paradoxically, an old friend," but "he was manifesting pretty literal paranoid behavior." In 1969, his last year in Buffalo, he sat down to write the final journal of this collection. It is in a leather ledger with yellow pages, written in tight, cramped script, and the title on the first page is *The Turned-Down Mouth*. It is as searing a read as the 1966 journal, flecked with moments of light and brilliance. It ends with a simple list of names and places, "Stars Seen in Person."

A few months after completing this last journal, Wieners was institutionalized again, this time for six months at a public hospital on Long Island. He started an enduring and generative friendship with Boston gay liberation activist and teacher Charles Shively, and kept the journal published as *A New Book From Rome*. After his release, he moved back to the Boston suburbs and survived the deaths of Charles Olson, Steve Jonas, and his mother Anna. He continued to develop new poetry, and worked on another journal, *Book of Prophecies*, building towards a tremendous, challenging book of new poems called *Behind the State Capitol, or the Cincinnati Pike*, published by Shively's Good Gay Poets Press in 1975. By this time he had settled into a comfortable but hand-to-mouth life at 44 Joy

Street, just a few blocks from the apartment on Grove where he lived while writing *The Untitled Journal of a Would-Be Poet.* The neighborhood had changed mightily, and so had he. He lived there for almost three decades, and by all accounts never stopped writing.

A NOTE ON THE TEXT

In the interest of readability, these journals are presented in a clear text format, meaning that the vagaries of the page—cross-outs, insertions and emendations, rearranged passages—have been judiciously resolved. A few of Wieners' especially provocative or revealing textual changes have been preserved. Errors within the prose that are very clearly accidental (a keystroke slip, for example) have been silently corrected; whenever there's been doubt, and whenever it appears within poetry, the apparent error has been left intact. Wieners was constantly revising his poems, but also studiously preserved textual accidents as integral to the meaning and prosody; in a 1963 letter to publisher Robert Wilson, he wrote that any "mistakes in grammar, punctuation and spelling" were "intentional, or absolute, as this is what the poem demanded . . ."

> That is true to the experience of the poem. The punctuation is right, as is the spelling, viz: *surrended* for *surrendered*; a comma at the end of a poem instead of a period; poems with no titles; or sentences beginning with small, lower-case letters. I hope this doesn't offend you.

And so, all eccentricities in spelling or usage within this book are preserved intentionally.

ACKNOWLEDGMENTS

All journals appear with permission of the Estate of John Wieners, whose literary executor Raymond Foye is a generous and untiring champion of his work.

The Untitled Journal of a Would-Be Poet is published courtesy of the John Wieners Papers, Special Collections Research Center of Syracuse University Libraries, with special thanks to Nicolette Dittrich and Lucy Mulroney.

Blaauwildebeestefontein and *A House In The Woods—Moths At The Window* both reside in the John Wieners Papers in the Special Collections of the University of Delaware Library, where Curtis Small has been of invaluable assistance.

Untitled 1969 Journal is held in the John Wieners Papers at the University of Buffalo Library. Special thanks to James Maynard, who has helped this project on numerous occasions, and to my John Wieners research comrade Robert Dewhurst, who first alerted me to its existence.

To thank Ammiel Alcalay is like thanking ink and paper, but I still want to thank *el capitán*.

This project was made by possible by the generous support of the Center for the Humanities at the Graduate Center of the City University of New York, under the inspiring leadership of Aoibheann Sweeney and support of Sampson Starkweather and Kendra Sullivan. I am eternally in their debt.

~~n~~ight is again Monday and Rita is outside washing my dishes.

, I have written that because Marie was here to tell me of her love

~~f~~ God. Seventeen is the most ~~h~~mind-breaking age. Tonight a machine from

~~whe~~re I work was here an~~d~~ the two girls came with him~~s~~. Marie was at her

~~bes~~dest. She went into a long solioquoy about having~~life~~ been a lady

~~wre~~stler and the~~n~~ ~~argued~~ ~~read~~ ~~with~~ ~~him~~ ~~about~~ ~~his~~ ~~poor~~ ~~w~~ife who had to go

~~out~~ and give bru~~sh~~ ~~demonstrations.~~ ~~Rita~~ ~~(we~~ ~~called~~ ~~her~~ Greta) took

the role of ~~my~~ ~~mistress,~~ ~~we~~ ~~talked~~ ~~about~~ ~~the~~ ~~gas~~ ~~bill~~ and the oatmeal

~~lef~~t in the morning dishes until night. She w ore my khakis and showed

~~my~~ sketches. He talked about his five children, Marie discussed busines~~s~~

~~at~~ the Casino burlesque house where she pretended to work and I informed

~~him~~ that I hated our mutual office. But now I amw ~~w~~riting and I feel tha~~t~~

~~I~~ must work on the new poem.

THE UNTITLED JOURNAL OF A WOULD-BE POET

And eight ~~shrill~~ *shrill* bel~~l~~s from Beacon Hill ~~ring~~ the world's not well
tonight,

—Tell of the killing of patient gulls ~~in filthyfull lagoons.~~

—Over agony who saves the tears, ✓

—Who carries back with arms full of nights
the hours that ~~were~~ shredded ~~away~~ *down by the imposing world*

Who remembers the desire,

and who will replace the subway womens' erased faces,

finding for them the years

when they braided blonde hair half~~,~~*halfamile*a-mile behind their backs,

who will fill the passion of garretteers,

who can _ive the girls who cannot ~~quite~~ grasp the real, fantasie~~s~~

of fabled knights who fight for fancy in an unreal Rome,

sending for~~t~~hem from the avenues where they last fell,

~~and~~ who will bring the battle boom and flags to broken legs

and who, besides the ever brooding bright eyes of death,

~~will wish we were home (will watch us home)~~ (will wish us home)

Tonight, on the 17th of January, nineteen hundred and fifty five, I begin the writing of what will be my intimate journal. Here, as the better dust blurbs shall say, are play reviews, people descriptions, impressions of my world, high nights and black nights. Here will be thoughts that I hope will sometime be poems, here will be stories, but most of all in this undisguised and true journal will be memories of the life I have chosen.

I ask you to bear with me here at the beginning as I have not written for such a long time, my head and heart grow tireder than my hands. Tonight is the coldest night of the year, and the cold kept the trees' branches un-quivering in the wind. I want to begin among the cold in my sixteenth year, the summer before I climbed the then immense and towering hill to what was called Boston College. They have since added some unsayable religious adjectives to its title. On the back of a swaying orange trolley, I turned a corner of Commonwealth Avenue, and growing over apartment houses the grey stalk of a Gothic tower. I cannot go into the early fears, the embarrassment, the self-consciousness of those first months under that tower, because every journal I have ever read devotes so much space to same that every journal reads the same. I shall tell of the boys I met there, the parties we went to that seemed to explode brighter than any parties in the world, the drunken afternoons, the tossing of Latin and Greek and French books into the air higher than anyone else had ever tossed Greek and Latin and French books. It was the time of one's life. Poetry was found at the first when a Jesuit priest called Leonard read Edna Millay's more discernible and youthful poetry in his best flaming twentiesh voice. It was

October of 1950 and She had died two days before and he read the last lines of "Moriturus:"

> "I shall bolt my door
>> With a bolt and a cable;
> I shall block my door
>> With a bureau and a table;
>
> With all my might
>> My door shall be barred.
> I shall put up a fight,
>> I shall take it hard.
>
> With his hand on my mouth
>> He shall drag me forth,
> Shrieking to the south
>> And clutching at the north.

He finished and looked up and said, "Edna Millay died two nights ago on the third step of her Steepletop staircase, collapsed over an empty wine glass. She didn't do much shrieking to the south and clutching at the north. But when I was in college, Edna Millay was what all the eager young girls were clutching to their bosoms and what all the bright young men were shouting through the parks."

> My candle burns at both ends,
> It will not last the night,
> But ah, my foes, and oh, my friends,
> It gives a lovely light!

Edna Millay was a goddess to me from that instant on. She is not a great poet, but she opened to me the avenues of great poetry. I was working as a student assistant in the College library for tuition and I took out her books (I still have some of them here to my guilt) and I labored over them. I did not understand them at first. The words made no sense, but neither did the articles in what I then thought were all the better magazines. I cut out pictures of her, I read everything about her, I brought her books years later even when I realized her great faults. The publication of "Mine the Harvest," her posthumous book of poems, sent me down the streets of Boston singing to myself, holding its shiny blue and chrome cover to my sides for joy. I made the buying of that book a ritual as I nearly do with all the books I buy; I brought the reading of her poems by Judy Anderson and still play them. P.207 of her Collected Lyrics is open in front of me now. Because of her I fell in love with the 1920s as I suppose all the country did from nineteen fifty on. I read F. Scott Fitzgerald's biography in <u>Life</u> and I began on Fitzgerald. His "Crack-Up" and Jay Gatsby and Zelda and all the disenchanted ones pulled me up by my hair. I nearly cracked inside wanting to drink bathtub gin and knock on speakeasy doors, and dance with insane young things who smoked in the back of subway cars and made love in fields of blue flowers. I read literal histories of the 20s by people like F. Lewis Allen (I think) and someone called Mark Sullivan. And the world came open now.

There grew from me big flowing worlds outside Milton, Massachusetts. Not all the people were the small, unbright ones that stood on the corner of Central Avenue and Eliot Streets. I would sit on Sunday afternoons in the sun on the brick wall outside an ice-cream factory and see the trolley cars shuttling into Boston and I remember saying, "someday, I will get on one of those all by myself and go in town, and something would run quick inside me and although I knew nothing of what I would find, the mystery of a world outside of the downtown Washington Street shopping center a world where I would know no one, where every shadow on a street corner was god, where bright, glistening women in white dresses went in and out of hotels all night long never let me rest in familiar patterns again. Neon lights made every face a face. Every eyebrow was remembered. I could tell how eyes would look at me. I would not let a face go by but I would tear into it until I made its eyes look into mine. Shadows were real, footsteps became men, laughter was white wine running down my throat. I did not want to laugh, I only wanted to hear laughing. I did not want to know what all the gaiety and the shouting was about, I only wanted genuine headless laughter running in my ears. I wanted bright faces not up against mine, I only wanted to watch bright faces go by. The widest streets I walked the most. Here I was freer. I did not like the Common and the Gardens except where the lamps came down and turned the trees into fire and the path was into gold streets. I haunted back and back again half-lit doorways, always watching to catch some little face of life that had a mask on it before. I loved windows with the curtains up and the people showing in them, bodies pressed against the window panes and even pieces of furniture that looked as if someone had just left them or was just going to return. But I was back in Milton and although I went through the city to school, I was always underground where the faces are not bright and glistening and where there are no white dresses and people only go in and out of men's rooms all night long. But it was beginning, and her poetry was my first vision, added onto the extra-curricular activities with the insane people I fortunately found in. Our first endeavor was the singing of Christmas Carols in the snow on the last day before vacation for the holidays. I had truly gotten drunk for the first time, it was with homemade Italian wine that someone had brewed for the holiday. We circulated paper cups in Latin class and poured from the great gallon jugs a liquid the taste of which I still remember every time I think of Horace. Fr. V.deP. O'B. as we called him developed the usual alcoholic gleam in his eye and let the class free to wander through the beginning snow, slipping and shouting, linking arms and feeling as defiant and dedicated as Christ. We advanced on a girls college miles out and smoked at all the prohibited places, were chased away by the black nuns sliding through the snow with their habits being turned and taken away by the wind. We came back for English at 3:30 and spent the hour with Leonard singing the same carols for the 25th time, and then plans were circled for a class Christmas party shortly before The Great Birth. It was again a snowy night and I remember the drug-store in Arlington Center with its enormous phallic monument outside dignifying everything around. I was the only one who actually came to the party. None of the other cars were able to maneuver in the storm or else older brothers advised fathers against it, but we, the hard core of perpetual celebrators, (seven of us) tramped to a lodge on the end of a lake, past iron fences, and down wet paths to wait but no one else came. A local boy invited us and the liquor to his home and we sang to his mother's accompaniment on the piano, kissed his lovely sister under the traditional mistletoe, urinated in the wrong basin and were sobered with the most penetrating black coffee ever brewed. It was more exhilarating than the previous liquor. Midyears came and the glamour of three-o'clock study sessions, endless cigarettes and arguments and theories and drives home as the sun was nearly coming over the visor passed me through my examinations except one. And then a minstrel show was sounded, and visiting ladies from the surrounding schools volunteered to dance in the chorus. It was show business for me, with rehearsals even for the chorus, learning lines and gestures, much activities and much singing on the backsteps of the library before morning classes and again the rides home with the rising sun and the cram of studies for the necessary marks. There was no discipline in us. Someone suggested, and immediately it was done. No matter what was asked, it was yes, yes, yes, now! And at last there were excursions into Boston or at least part of it. Someone had discovered a tavern called "The Ye Olde Garden Café" in the North End and it was and is our nostalgic meeting place. There, we met the woman with the erased face, the man who played songs with spoons on the tables, the little accordionist who sang "Sweet Rosie O'Grady," and "When Jaded Irish eyes are smilin." There was the shy dark boy who had one glass of beer and who on the way home ran over to a doorway and began urinating while everyone threw snowballs at him and the warehouse door. There was a snowball fight in Haymarket Square, in the middle of its streets, and in its underpasses. There was the waitress who served us at sixteen and seventeen although the laws read twenty-one and her fellow-waitress who wouldn't let you in until you were twenty-three. We had to decipher which were her nights off. There was a woman who waited & believed for her detective-husband every night in the bar next door and who danced the polka with me one night in the middle of Hanover Street and kissed me in a wicked way, but the most wicked thing of all was when years later I was in a very elegant ice-cream parlor in Boston and a very elegant hostess shoved me to a corner booth, she completely forgotten that she ever danced a polka with me on a street in the shadow of North Station. Her hair was a different color and her clothes were cleaner and there was no wicked gleam in her nowdull eyes.

end of January 17, 1955

Begin

Second entry- January 18th, 1955.
Today will be a hard night for the proverbial golden people are coming with their beercases and their loud laughing. I love loud laughing. I shall write my three hours, I shall write my three hours, I shall. Despite the loud laughing in the next room, I shall. Today was a routine day "at the office". I was five minutes late and it took thirty minutes of my waking eternity to worry about this. I had an hour lunch and I read Gerald Manley Hopkins for three-quarters of it. "Startle the poor sheep-back in the ship wreck . . ." is an excellent line. It had the tremendous running lines of a wave. This past week-end has been the most exhilarating time of my existence in

Boston. Friday evening began with preparations for the typical six o'clock dinner and the first front door suddenly sounded and a girl who I had never met but once and her suitcase were outside it. At a party in Providence I had invited her to come to my city and spend a week-end and she, carried by an impulse, and wanting to be free of her easel for a few days, came. Her name is Pat and she dresses in the oldest clothes available for since she was always the smart one and her younger sister the pretty one, she has never tried to compete for beauty. She avoids lovely hangings and silks for she feels embarrassed by them. She has immense black hair which she holds back from her face which wears no makeup. She paints for life and attends the Rhode Island School of Design. She slept with me for fifteen minutes at about three Saturday night but then crawled over me and spent the last hours of the night reading Virginia Woolf's "Orlando" and eating crackers and peanut butter, finally falling asleep at about 7:30 only to wake me at 11. She served me ice-cream in bed for my breakfast and wanted to return to Providence immediately to sleep for something she said, near sixteen hours and take a long hot bath as I have no hot water and the bathroom doesn't work. She found this out by flooding it all over the unwaxed floor at about four, Sunday morning. But before starting on Saturday, I must write about Rita. Rita is a girl I met on a Tuesday evening at the Museum of Arts on Huntington Avenue. We went to Rodin and The Flight of Love, we walked in eight rooms of Greek and Roman remains, caressing the head of Augustus with its slivered and shattered leftside, its only beautiful side. I wanted to kiss Augustus' lips like I had done before but I was not able and did not dare. We went to a lecture on the Minoans and overseas empire and left when the lights went down, came home on the crowded trolley together, exchanged addresses in the nightmare glare of the Park Street subway station, and left each other for what I thought was for an ever. The same evening that Pat came with her Pisarro and

Picasso, her trunk containing Pall Malls, and sketching paper and India Ink and a skirt, there was another sound at the first front door and it was again Rita with her plain face and the extraordinary eyes and mouth. She left and Pat and I went to the Boheme hangout, the only Bohem hangout in the city where she sketched and drew wide attention, while I drew mad poems in my head because of the bronze magic of their beer. I met Rita as planned and my insides were open for some reason and I told her what she must do to find Beacon Hill. That sounds like snobbery and I can't help it. I am beating these keys for my lack of words to describe how she looked at me, how her arms were pushed tight together, how her red and black checkered coat hung over her bare arms, how her hips stood out against her corduroy skirt, how her cheek felt against my hard cheek, how, when she asked me what and how I regarded people and if I felt sorry for most of them as she did, I told her of seeing a drunken bleached woman staggering over Boylston Street on its wide sidewalks, how I wanted to run up behind and take her up by her arms and put her in a safe taxi or a chair or give her good warmth, and I was afraid, and all I could murmur, was God Love YOU, God love YOU, God love YOU, and then I thought, There is no God, so my love love you and keep you warm, and I finished and she turned and looked at me and said "I love you," with her pure voice on the you and no one has ever said it to me like that before, with all my guards down, with no wiles, she told me how she has been inside crying and nearly crying now and I told her that she would never be lonely for I would think of her as I am thinking of her now, and she said she wished she could live with me, and I said we could read together and study and walk near each other. She left but will be back soon and the world of the spirit will be open for us, which is sometimes so much more orgiastic than the world of the body, but god's world brings its ecstasy to me too, but it is lazy ecstasy of the animal, while it is the afterglow of the spirit that will send you screaming, like I am nearly screaming now, in this study, typing on white pieces of paper how much I want to see Rita Nolan again, because it is again Tuesday and we walked last Tuesday through Tudor rooms and eighteenth century rooms and tapestry halls and augustan remains. Great love always comes to me on Tuesdays, god's love came first to me on Tuesday but his was the body kind while hers will be the mind. His also is now the mind. They have come and so I will have to fight against the coming into their goldenness, but I shall, for if I go out into the living room with them I will not be a writer, I will only be the enjoyer and I am tired of enjoying. This is the only peace, this is why I run home at night, cutting across the frozen lagoon in the garden, passing the bright shops where I spent the mad hours, but it is brighter and more mad here, filling up the white paper with grey print. I will finish the entries for tonight but I just remembered that I have not finished with Pat Sloan the painter from Providence yet and so I shall. With all the glow of Friday night on me, someone called Earle Pilgrim had sketched my picture and it made me glad and I had been happy in my sevens, or in my cups. They are going to win over, I am going to go out. I will not, even though the cigarettes have gone out and there are no matches and the glass had fallen onto the floor and my stockings are wet, I will not, at least not for a while, at least not for a while. Their music is loud and they are talking of Emily Bronte and I am tortured by them, my nerves want to go out and laugh with them, and I am screaming to go out with them. I shall talk about Pat tomorrow night, I cannot go with this tonight, they are too much. I shall try the only true thing I want to do. I shall go to my poems.

End of entry for January 18, 1955, a poor one I am afraid.

It is a cold and not very mad Wednesday, the 19th and I come back to Pat Sloan. I did the three hours yesterday despite them. We left in the snow the wrong side of Beacon Hill to do the

Museums and be very artz-craftz, me in torn sneakers and faded elegance, she with her suitcase of Pall Malls. It was noon and we took a beer at the sevens although the lady wanted soda-water. This at the sevens is completely unheard of, where everything to be anything must be either a 15¢ split or a glass of dark beer, please, but Pat asked for gingerale or soda water. The bar I took her to after this to the Charles St. meeting house which is a church of all religions therefore of none. As a giant backdrop behind the altar, containing nothing but full bookshelves, the pastor has hand painted a wall mural attempting to depict the universe. It is a blue & silver painting of the earth's orbit ornamented with Christmas stars & milky ways. It has come to me now that the church is officially Universalist. Over the cream-colored pews hang the bronze symbols of every religion existent. She was fascinated but since I had been there twice before, less hungover than that morning, I sat on her green suitcase in a hallway and pantomimed ½ of The Thinker and the bride widowed at the hotel, and the other half my role of poet with sunken cheeks and inturned toes. We said I would make an excellent photograph of tragedy. We stopped at the Personal Book shop further on Charles Street and afterwards Pat told me how she sometimes steals books and I told her that I did too but we were both trying to free ourselves of the habit. She offered to take the book I was coveting if I would donate the money towards her purchasing of Untermeyer's "Modern British and American Poetry." I declined and she was glad because she was trying to get from the habit. We went over the frozen lagoon of the Public Gardens in my frozen sneakers, and walked the turning white streets filled with scurrying and hunched up people. We passed a florist and I offered to buy her the violets in the window if only I had the money, but she said that winter violets were horrible because of the price, but the thought made her happy, warm, and beautiful (I stop for a minute for some silly dance tune is coming in the blinded window and makes my heart think of something different than a frozen lagoon.) The ship's whistle from off the Charles brings me back again to the scurrying junks sliding along Arlington Street as we ran from the cold on all its red brick sidewalks. Again I took her to a bookshop, the Book Clearing House, its book sidewalk stalls out in the snow on Boylston, and we wandered for an hour in the rows of new and rotting books with our stomachs rolling. After tossing half of a silver dollar four times and having it come down with the lady up all four times, I brought, with 2 of my last 3 dollars, "The Collected Poems of Richard Aldington," and Pat brought a little new magazine with Orson Welles on the cover as Macbeth, called "Film Culture." I read a weekly on the store's second-floor window sill high over the bright wide sidewalks. We had luncheon at Hayes Bickford and since everything that we could afford they had sold, Pat had a cup of black coffee and I ate a fried egg in a bun. We stole a discarded roll and butter off a waitress's tray and as I was taking down surreptitiously an apple for Pat off the window display, Pat brought two glasses of tomato juice even though I had suggested we take two glasses of water and mix ketchup in them as I have seen done many places many times. To prove this, I imagine, was why she brought the tomato juice. Enriched, we set off on the subway to the Museum, Pat giving me a dollar for subway fares. It is hard here to describe what the next hour and one half was. I spent most of it looking at Pat, a truer masterpiece as she stood in front of the Matisses and the Degas, with her head almost bowed, her hair touching the canvasses, her dirty little fingers running over the paint stroked softly. "Her breath came short and scarce at all." Here I don't want to be the usual would-be wit writing for his audience. I only want to set down as I felt it the picture of that ridiculous girl standing in tribute before her gods. Catalogue of prints/ She charged over to me some of the love that she was pouring over the white and gold and red marks on the Renoirs and Matisses. There is an adjoining museum in the Fenway, the madwoman Isabella Stewart Gardner's home. and in her

13

courtyard great orchid and yellow flowers bloomed. From the third story, it seemed as if violin strings were chanting over ancient and delicate songs. She left me in Park Street with the promise that some Saturday morning very soon she will bring her bicycle on the train and a plentiful picnic lunch minus beer and ice-cream and black coffee, and we would tour the museums for forever. A great band of red light, seeming to be a river width, and backdropping the churches and insurance company steeples took me out over the Common in the cold and kept me singing at the goodness of living in a tenement on the top of one of Boston's seven hills, surrounded with ship's whistles and custom house horns and friends with their heart in their eyes.

—

OMIT → Sunday evening, the night before the first entry, was spent with a friend of five years, Robert Greene, being intimate with each other by talking of our loves and passions, our books and musics. This all brings me up to today and so for tomorrow I shall have to go into the past and recreate and redance the hours of my not altogether-lost youth. With my existence bearing me along as it has been for the five years, I can die easy. Despite its hundred heavy weights of longing and foolish dreams, all the agony has been worth it. ~~God is knocking at the door and in a minute it will kiss and wrap its blond arms around me. Now, I leave this paper for god.~~

—

Short entry for Thursday, the 20th. Rita was here from 600 to midnight. I came home eager for mail and as I opened the bottom door off the street some one else opened the glass paned hall door five steps above me, and in smiles and fascinating hair bobbing, it was she or her with a black

14

notebook in her hand and her voice saying I was just about to leave. I was unable to say anything. We read poetry, Millay's and Wilde's and Shakespeare. And at 930, the people came. They came with their small talk and their Tasso and indoor tennis and I opened the sonnets and pointed out the words, Oh, to be alone, to shut the door and be alone again. They would not leave us alone, they would not go, I am eaten by their words again, their words of nothingness, on and on and my hand could only touch her brown quilted skirt and my fingers, sometime touching hers for a minute but always their eyes were on us, watching and saying "who is he playing a game with," and always her green eyes asking to be alone, just to read again the horrible reality of the unending minutes crushing out the little magic of the world. There is no loveliness in the real world, it is transitory, the beautiful minute is fleet, it is gone to the world it came from before one is even able to touch it and one never knows when or where it is, afterwards one says, it was here and I did not even know, and it goes, and all the longing is back for it to come again, it is the unreal second, maybe this is it now, maybe the desire is the fulfillment, the goodbye the beginning, all else is grey and dust covered, choking over one's eyes, up one's nostrils. She gave me a pastel sketch in blue and I asked her its name and she said that she hated to classify things, that she could never remember what she read as she never paid any attention to title or author. We should not want to know what everything's name is. Over my desk (you go about the world today in disgust) is a card of a stone maiden holding a naked youth in her arms. Her strong great gold fingers are holding his naked thigh and there is consolation here which is not Here. Here, there is no refuge, not even in poetry for my soul has been laden over with the lead of my life. I shall try to burn away reality, I shall piece out the dross and try for the purity of something that I do not know. Is it in words that I discover my reality I must go far away, go into oblivion and find the steepletops and the towers of [illeg] and Rapallo. Somewhere is aloneness that I cannot face alone and if I bring any one with it, it has gone into the companionship that kills. I am not satisfied with what I am and shall be mad if it goes on with the same fervor that is burning me now, O confusion you are prevalent. I again can do no more, I am again submerged in sterility. Not even her memory can soothe me now, I am the artificial, this sweet hell, that is a quote from someone that we read tonight. I never understood as well as tonight Whitman's "Out of the Cradle endlessly rocking." There seems no doubt that Mr. Whitman actually found his flag in that he-bird, the solitary guest from Alabama. I am not clear, I do not see the words as they should be spoken, I am too? Is this humility and is this clearness and a true vision of my inadequacy? Am I? If only the poetry would come that I want to come, but I am afraid that I will not be a poet, I will not sing the solitary songs that are I know in me to sing. I must sing but I am not able, it will not come as the others? but in the others' poems have I read have I been satisfied? Pound and Shakespeare and Eliot to a lesser rank, yes! Pound, yes, Pound. I do not know his Cantos yet, but "Personae" is the type of poetry that must be said but what can one say now after he has done it. He has started the Rigisorgimento and yet, in some country, some dirty town, in the poverty of loneliness, utter, I will utter the songs for this Risorgimento. Utter to the full greatness that I realize Poetry needs, Yes I shall put it in capital letters for It is there to be capitalized. I cannot stand your wittiness, your phrase for everything, your books of quotable quotes, your incessant realizations of how you are affecting everyone. Everyone does not matter. It is the capital letters that matter. I shall go until my fingers come out of the bones. and I shall keep crying the same cries until I have said what I must, for it must be said or death shall cover up my brain, in rituals of routine from the mechanics of the machine heart.

     End of entry for the 20th.

In this I am again in retreat, yes, you shall be solace, I cannot face the skyscrapers or the culture that you talk about. I will not bring what ever I have to you. I cannot stand the reality of you. I cannot stand the world as it is, and to escape, in my best dramatical words, I shall turn to the poetry of unreality. I do not want to be real. I do not want to have fingers and lust and food. I want to stand over wide-open windows over the streets and see the realities go by and not be one. I will look at the unseen clouds that you cannot see. I want dreams to be reality, I want imagination to be my weekly pay envelope. I do not want to sit and talk about the penal system in Massachusetts or the rising cost of life, I want to read poetry to frightened girls who run to me with their souls out, waiting to be fed from my soul. I do not want their bodies, I do not want anybody's body, or blonde hair, I want to fall in love with a girl skating, wrapped in my overcoat under the lights from a green bridge. I want to chase a pair of white skates over grey ice, skates that I can never quite catch up with, I do not want breakfast and dinner and census-taking and electric-light bills, I want little books in bright colors that are written in brighter colors on the black print inside. I want to stand in front of phantoms and let my voice fill their journeying souls. This tonight I believe and I want every night to believe it, I do not want it to fade in the reality of tomorrow's dawn or the ecstasy of tonight's body, I want to be dream. Every man to me seeks a desired perfection, every man goes to his own good, it does not matter if it be for murder or rape or money, each man nonetheless seeks a good, and thus there must be somehow a kind of good which shall fill this. Death shall bring the answer, whether death is dying or the beginning of life, it shall still bring the answer. The questioning shall be over, the seeking done. Thus we <u>should</u> love the love that all men seek, we cannot love men as they are, but see them in their possible and final beauty. To hold this unreality of my soul against those, who when they see vitality and belief would gnaw it out, and destroy you to bring you up or down to where they are. Am I neurotic to think this? There are many who will do just this, does each man kill the thing he loves, no, but the lover or the hater can sometimes kill by love the fire alien to their fire which the lover thinks burn in the loved one's heart. Protect me from this, death, my god, my Jesus Christ, oblivion or birth, it does not matter what death brings of the two, but the searching shall be over. Is that all, love asks, when you give the fire of your lips, for love wants the other fire, love wants to kill the alien flaming, love wants to make you loved and nothing else, and this is sterility . . . might I sometime find the maze to "breathe out sonnets on the midnight air," to feel inside not something that I can write a poem about, but something that a poem must be written about. No imitation, but new, as the new back of stamps, that will hold to anything, even the palms of your hands, Christ's hands were pierced, I read somewhere, and I looked at cliffs and clouds with quiet eyes, and as of some elf, singing sweet songs to please himself, and let us go then, and all the trivia of the poets that I must cleanse out so that I will be washed, receptive, observer to the world that needs me somehow. I cannot write anymore, I cannot ever say the things that I once could say, am I burnt out have I been choked, is it all over now, the excitement and the labor, no, the labor is still, the capability is gone, that is why I run away from this typewriter, that is why there cannot be devotion on my part, why I have never written a poem, because I cannot, and I will exclamate it! The lights go up, for I see the other ones, the strugglers, the Hopkins and the Pounds, and they talk of birds build but not I build, send my roots rain, the words that come too goddam easy, the fighting for the fire to stay alive, for the labour and the excitement, and it may be, it is, I shall not despair, I shall not give up, I am trying the same game that the geniuses tried, that the immortal tried, I am in the tradition of Socrates and Augustine, and Donne, and Whitman, they are all my brothers, they worked at the same job that I am working, I am using their desks and their pencils, and they shall send me letters, I know it, to help me. They too wanted to say and could not, as I want to and can not, and I shall not give up, there is too much here to give up yet. Your voice came out for me trying over the typewriter

To touch me and to bring me to you.
It is the same with beauty, whatever that is,
it comes in over the rooftops at night
and we do not see or hear,
and we turn to each other, and say
I am so unhappy, I wish I could see the moon again,
if that dreadful cloud would pass,
and the cloud,
trailing great gowns of felt and velvet grey,
is more beautiful.
I was writing my happiness, whatever that is,
and thought that <u>love</u>? would never come
and your voice came out
only reaching the typewritten.

End of entry for 21st the fridayevening-saturday morning.
    There is much screaming in the streets tonight, parties are going on all about these rooms. Girls' voices come drifting up in their threadlike sounds and "Hi Ho, my baby – – ˘ – – ˘ all night long.

There is a great slamming and starting of cars,
a going in and out, a night to stay up all night
and watch it all but I must go down and warm
and beat on the needy fires.

(and else true lights were the only warmth we had.)

the 22nd

Today or we should say the only part of today that mattered was spent with R. She is coming again Monday and she shall sit in the next room doing her work while I sit here and find the compensation for living. Today was the meeting of the Boston Chapter of the Poetry Society of England. I took a part in the dramatic reading of Chris Fry's "Venus Observed." The entire thing was shabby but it is wonderful to retreat into the 19th century or at least into what I imagine the 19th century should be. I am learning discipline, this is the sixth day without fail that I have spent in writing, realizing every day the true self here. I am beginning to think of myself as a practicing writer not just a potential. I have tried a new poem tonight and I shall go back, but the words torture to find, the emotion I have, but the lack of being able to bring out the inside, is pain.

It begins: And eight shrill bells on Beacon Hill ring the world's   not well tonight.

With her there is no compulsion, there is only the feeling, I cannot call it knowledge, that I am complete, not in the ecstatic way that is present when I am with god, but the closeness of souls that one can barely ever approach with others. Climbed the hill tonight a little drunk and nasty, carrying the voice of Marlene Dietrich under my arm which voice I would like to write a poem about. Something is started but it is not genuine yet. In tonight's poem, there is trueness for me, there are not the words I want to use but I shall write down the desire for true words here, if nothing else I shall picture the frustration and longing of the artist, if nothing else I shall picture the desire, possibly not the fullfillment (what an interesting word) full fill, why the combination. This is a word that can be worked on, filthy full, lust full (that has been done) I am so afraid of what has been. I want to go away. I want to leave this city and the hundred faces who come looking to me for entertainment. I want to find loneliness, and yet tonight, to Rita, I said that this was the happiest This was the happiest days . . . these were the happiest days of my life, so I cannot go away, I do not have the strength to suffer the loneliness that cannot be shared, at least shared with other lonelies (W.H. Auden). Rita said tonight, "Write, write for me through you, write my writing for me." God tells me always to write and yet above this he is great mindbreak (new word, good) for his demanding from me of things I cannot give him. God asked me last night about this journal and I told him that I would never let anyone read this, at least I know not for years, and he said he knew why, because I said bad things about him in it, I suppose I do, but I cannot have obligation. The Brunswick Hotel was built in 1873. I have been told that Henry James had the room with the third floor corner windows and that I knew was an ideal place for the viewing of Copley Square which is so much the true Boston. The only part of Boston which matters is a small section of Park Street, the Common, disregarding the ball field, all of Beacon Street up, to Dartmouth, the Public Gardens, Beacon Hill, all of the streets running from Arlington Street past Copley Square, the grand old facades on Commonwealth Avenue. The Brunswick was once a grand hotel, where young girls would go out and buy something wonderfully new to wear at its receptions. The owls on its outside stairways once had red eyes that were lit at night by pulling cords that hung about their necks. It is a brownstone building and today its lobby is filled with shining red leather chairs and painted kelly green for the Irish. It is shabby now and filled only with shriven old ladies who remember when they went out to buy something wonderfully new for its receptions. Today they have a sidewalk café populated by the summer theatre stars and a Cub room where Calypso dancers are painted on the walls and here there are yellow leather chairs. But still in its hallways are great old rust colored marble statues of mothers with children, and maidens with god-men, and mosaiced floors and great marble tiles in the men's rooms. The old women know where to come and die, they come there because here, it is still Boston, and they are treated with courtesy and honor as if their civilization had not lost a great deal when their horses were taken away. Here old actresses, even at eighty-six are frowned upon because they paint their nails and their cheeks too obviously. But still the old women hold their afternoon teas, and flute solos and poetry drift again through the marble halls and lost pink carnations are found again, but soon, the last of these old women shall be carried out and the Sweeney's and the O'briens and the Nolans will come and paint the marble statues kelly green, and after their race has been laid out too, what will the Brunswick, if there is still a Brunswick, hear in place of an old woman wrapped in grey long furs reading her poetry in a crackled voice, talking of lemon verbena and morning glory and the great sleep which will wash the Brunswick clean. Tomorrow I will reread the 19 and a ¼ pages that I have typed since Monday, and the sixty three hundred approximate words I have typed this fabled past six days.

I wanted to wipe you away with sleep
and there on the bed was the sweat from your forehead,
the matted outline of your arms,
your thighs, your back, your legs.
I got under softly so the sheets would not be moved.

the 24th

Tonight is again Monday and Rita is outside washing my dishes. You, I have written that because Marie was here to tell me of her love for god. Seventeen is the most mind-breaking age. Tonight a machine from where I work was here and the two girls came with him. Marie was at her wildest. She went into a long soliloquy about having been a lady wrestler and then sympathized with him about his poor wife who had to go out and give brush demonstrations. Rita (we called her Greta) took on the role of my mistress, we talked about the gas bill and the oatmeal left in the morning dishes until night. She wore my khakis and showed her sketches. He talked about his five children, Marie discussed business at the Casino burlesque house where she pretended to work and I informed him that I hated our mutual office. But now I am writing and I feel that I must work on the new poem.

> And eight shrill bells from Beacon Hill the world's not well
> tonight,
> -Tell of the killing of patient gulls.
> -Over agony who saves the tears,
> -Who carries back with arms full of nights
> the hours that shredded down by the imposing world
> Who remembers the desire,
> and who will replace the subway women's erased faces,
> finding for them the years
> when they braided blonde hair halfamile behind their backs,
> who will fill the passion of garreteers,
> who can give the girls who cannot grasp the real, fantasies
> of fabled knights who fight for fancy in an unreal Rome,
> sending for them from the avenues where they last fell,
> who will bring the battle boom and flags to broken legs
> and who, besides the ever brooding bright eyes of death,
> (will wish us home)

Tuesday the 25th

This must be a short entry again for I am weary tonight, not only in my body, but weary from being awake and thinking about nothing too much.

And tomorrow and tomorrow and tomorrow, all over again, the grimy green office where I must work, the little bug-men that I just work with. Yet always the thought comes, this is only because I am tired, I shall sleep, and tomorrow will be better. Why is there a tomorrow. I did not do much of anything on my poem, I doubt until I sit down here that I should continue with poetry, and then my hope begins to be cleared by thinking on this paper. Already there is the warm beginning of thought that this is what gives meaning to life. This is why I might be here. This answers M. I am here to fill a spiritual reservoir from which the future writers of the world might slake their thirst, i.e. if I myself become a writer and keep to the discipline, avoid the easy escapes. I have been moderately successful this time, and it is the first time, and so I use that to keep the battle running up-hill. One can find so many shining diversions, a ten-cent beer, a new singer at the 76, a cup of tea with a warm friend, an answer to a knock on the door, or just abandonment to the passing moment. I am driven, but that drive is what might make me finally become the longed for, the needed, adjective writer. In Boston is nearly my whole world, the world where all my friends are, where the streets are more known to me than my home streets. I went there tonight, and saw the "family" again. I feel lonely for them, for my mother because her whole world has nearly left her. She is surrounded now by her pots and pans and many beds, and there is no one to cook in the pans for and no one to change the sheets for. There is only my father who never existed for her or if he did, quickly shot himself in her mind. The world is full of my mothers and fathers, lonely men and women, who give themselves to their children because there is nothing else for them, just as I try to give myself to this, feeling that there is barely, except god and my lovely (what an insincere word) friends. The children grow needy and dependent and then leave, as I have done, to find those things to attach themselves to, and it is only the few cursed or blessed ones who can discover the spiritual detachment, which will not leave them until their "souls" do. This weekend will be spent in New York and it will be hectic, the theater will take up most time I hope, and not the faceless, ever full bars. I would like to try to write of New York of its glittering, but so many have tried. I have only found F. Scott Fitzgerald and Ezra Pound in the few lines from his "Mia Patria" to adequately do it. Soon, I will go there and live for a few weeks. And soon, how many more months of that machine existence must I endure, I will go to the museums and concerts of Boston again, back to the libraries and the theatres, that offer the comfort found only from the tiny parts of the world. I feel alive and awake again, I could go on for another two hours, there is strength here that I never truly found before. This, I must say it again is my reality, this tiny, wordless, province is the found horizon of my life . . . I wish though that all the interferences and weaknesses on my part, the grimy, finger detaining, body heating weaknesses would grow old, or be exhausted, but they always return, not with added strength but with the same illusion-shattering strength that they always have had. The only answer is to develop the walls and barrier within myself.

End of entry, short but somehow consoling, of January 25, 1955.

Wednesday, the 26th.
What can explain the tragedy of this world? If anyone asks me why I can only write on the tragic themes, I shall surely answer, Is there any other? Has life any other theme but a tragic one? Is it only longing, pierced but the hope that cannot last. Tonight, I saw a beautiful grey-haired woman lying on a green bandana in the gutter of Tremont Street, waiting for an ambulance or death to carry her off to consolation. But the hope was there, another woman bent down as a song and fixed the bandana and seemed to stroke somehow the woman's pain. On the swaying train, coming into Park Street, a woman in a brown, soft cloth, pushed through the crushed throng with her hand to her mouth. As the door opened, she crouched, and I saw the face of a bleached blonde girl, waiting to get on, turn away, her forehead wrinkling up under the make-up. R. Greene is here, sitting outside talking about his Veronique to Gilbert. They are coming here for the week-end while I am in New York.

I hope to get to the Poetry Center while I am in the "white and glittering" city. I feel somehow devoid of thought today. I would rather go off and read Pound's poetry in a corner, or listen to Bizet. A very sympathetic article has appeared in the Atlantic Monthly by Archibald MacLeish, titled "The Poet as Playwright". It is devoted mainly to the criticism of T.S. Eliot's view on the theatre and the use of poetry in it. Eliot feels that poetry discerned as such in the theatre is a dramatic convention and that it renders to the theatre-goer the illusion of the artificial. MacLeish says in effect that Eliot advocated the theory that the stage attempts to depict life as it is, rather than a new creation of life, which all art should be, we both believe. Art has to be a new creation. It has to be like birth, that is, it has to be as striking to the onlooker as a new world is. As W.C.W repeats over and over again, in his poetry, not a copy of nature but a creation. I have had a story running over and over again in my mind concerning a man who rides the swan boats. These hold the same fixation for him as alcohol or sex would to another. His wife tries to understand. As he comes home late, she questioning, reveals, that he has been doing so well, staying away from the swans for nearly three weeks now, while the reader knows that the man is late because he had ridden the boats until nearly dark, and had only stopped because the dark had come on, and the passengers left. But that night, she finds the overlooked ticket stub in his pocket and some kind of a scene follows where all his past faults are revealed, how he couldn't hold a job because he was always late from lunch, even when he worked downtown in the shopping area, he would rush through the Common, through the contented lunchtime crowds, and plan to stay for only one ride through the lagoon but once he got on, he was unable to get off. They even had a charge account for him. The pay-check sometimes almost completely went for this. One year, he had stayed away for nearly seven weeks but one of his children had heard so much talk about the swans that he whined that he wanted to ride them. And they went. On the surface, he was calm, but the first chance he could, on the first false pretext, he fled back. After this, she left him bitterly, she sent him a card at Christmas with wild swans on it, and gloated because she knew that the lagoon was frozen and the swans caged, and the boats in dock. With the next spring, he was the first there. He got a room in the corner house on Commonwealth Avenue, so he could see them with spy glasses from his room at night. And then the little money that was left from his insurance was nearly gone, and he sold his blood, and after they refused him for safety, he turned to beggaring, and then one day without food and no shelter, his clothes in tatters about him, he ran through the park for the last time. He had snatched a woman's purse from Tremont Street and took a dollar from it, threw the contents of it into the face of three little shop-girls who were pointing at him running up the street, and then entering the gardens, very calmly, paid the man for four tickets and sat in the last row, watching the children dragging their fingers in the yellow-brown water, listened to the mothers admonishing the children dragging their long fingers in the yellow water and as the boat rounded the small ideal island in the center of his only world, with the three unused pieces of pink paper in his hand, he slid from the boat with a small splash, just where the water came over his head.

Tonight is truly the coldest of the year. R. is in the next room reading Saroyan's "The Beautiful People" a play which is a re-affirming of the individual and his goodness. When I am with her, I do not want to be stationary. I want to go out into Boston, and see people and have people see her. It might be that I feel inadequacy when I am with her, or it could be that I have wanted to fulfill so many longed for experiences, sights, paintings, and people with someone like her, that I cannot waste time, doing the ordinary things. Veronique is coming here Friday from Providence, after I have left for N.Y. She shall stay the week-end, and how I want to see her again. It shall be great joy to me when some of the people from Providence come to Beacon Hill and make it their home. I want this to be a center, I want to make Boston a literary mecca, and have people walk its curves and twists in the same enchantment that I sometimes do. I think R. is not reading as thoroughly as she should as I hear the pages turn too rapidly, but I must not look for her faults, I feel such an emptiness in front of her mind, not that she is especially bright, but that she wants to hold tight the brightness that she thinks I offer, and I do not. I am a domestic in front of her, I mop floors and wash out bathtubs. It is only here writing, that I make for myself the gaudy and the "fabulous" that people think is a part of me. After the excitement of my being on the train tomorrow fades, I shall try to write something to describe my impressions of hurtling to the greatest, or should we call it the grandest city in the world. One needs or one thinks he needs gigantic quantities of money to approach N.Y. I have always thought that and this shall be one of the few times that I have gone there to enjoy its theatres and its museums alone, without having to drink up every bar I see. The same old bar faces, the tragic, fascinating bar faces.

I should stay here and write but I want to go out to Rita very much and read Pound's poetry to her. She says that she loves to hear me read, she is the first one to say this & I do not think she listens to the words but only to the sound of my voice, which I am not quite sure I would like her to do. I would rather be caught away with the poetry itself, like A. Landy (subconsciously I wanted his last name here, for I suppose I am writing this for the future to read. Doesn't every writing person write for the future to read?) I think that a moment of pureness is going to come to us tonight, we have been building slowly, not talking very much, and when we do, losing something, but there seems to be an openness on both our parts for something like hope and courage to come here tonight. "The office" is worse today, and I was possessed for the first time, the longest time that I have not been possessed with this in my job history, to walk to the coat-rack, put on faded elegance and desert them for the streets. I did that once at Gilchrist's and I was in near-ecstasy for a night.

1:15 Same entry.

I have just seen her off, she rode in a taxi home because she is late, and the hope and the courage did come, that is why I am writing now. We laid beside each other on the living-room rug, with a gold stitched blue pillow under our heads, that I bought in the Morgan Memorial for 20¢, and we talked about what our "love" is, we have decided that it shall not be physical, even though that seems to be what we are drawn to. We shall sacrifice that for the greater joy of our spiritual love, without quotations this time. There is no such thing but love in the spiritual sense, for in the body sense, it comes out only as desire or the need of love, but not the fullness and the elation that can be found in the soul, or whatever they are calling it. She knows I am having a physical affair now, but knows not with whom. I have been so happy tonight and still am, even though up till midnight I had ruined it by running out to the Dunn's apartment and down to the 7's, and seeing people and planning with people. Can we go on? Won't I be bored with it after a night or a week, won't I be looking around in bars for the physical people, won't it all shatter. Maybe I can not keep away from my own physical self, like no one else can, but with her, I shall not let it win, the soul is greater, she said, it can win over the dying body. Over our bodies together, it can win, but not over the others.

It is Friday, January 28th. This is the silver train to New York. We have a smoking car, a grill car, a bar car, and no doubt a little boy and girl's bar. The seats in this train are filled with all the clean young people that one sees in college towns. There are three men over sixty in this car. One of them has chosen me and on his way home, he works industriously on a daily computation sheet for the Austin Company, Builders and Engineers. He wears a black blue suit with a red stripe in it. The suit has a vest and he wears it. Doubtless, this is a two pant suit, but I cannot say yet whether he wears these. There is a gold watch chain spread across his belly. I am going to eat the ham sandwich which I have brought with me now, and we shall record his reaction. Ah yes, across his lap is the Reader's Digest and he is chewing gum. He has begun reading now, "Close Up of Herbert Hoover, Jr." in condensation.

Three seats up on the right are two college girls, painted, blonde, undoubtedly from Pembroke in Providence, a painted blonde college. They are playing cards, but continually (He's begun the Providence Evening Bulletin) they jump up and their little ridiculous eyes look over the rest of the car, for their audience. The car is 80% sailors. They put three coats on the overhead racks, stretching their breasts to bursting each time. Their scarfs, three trunks and many books are put up, each with equal strain. He is itching now, and the ham is gone, he ignored it, pausing only once to brush off its invisible crumbs from his blue suit.

On this train time, I was going to write continually. I have slept for fifteen minutes, had two cups of water, three cigarettes, a magazine, stared at people and their bodies, and was stared at. And now we are past the proverbial New Rochelle, are past Mount Vernon and are stopping for a town whose name I am not do not bother to find out. (It is 125th Street.)

This is New York. Time, up but I do not have a man from Austin Company down. Brunettes are hurrying their light brown coats on, sailors are rushing or more accurately marching through. Under a light, I just saw a blackboard with 117th Street printed on it in white letters. The brunette across from me, wearing the light brown coat and cream colored glasses, is sitting on the edge of her blue felt seat. She is twisting into her hands a magazine "How An American Girl Can Make Good in Paris" and her hands are very long, thin with painted nails at the end of them. I have thrown away a Christmas tie from around my neck under the seat. I saw a sign in white saying Manhattan Savings Bank. A band playing? We have stopped at 95th Street. Conductors are opening all the doors shouting over, don't ever stop shouting over and over, nine-tee-fif-thsteet, ni-intee-fifthst-reeet-ah. There are great lights outside every window. We seem to be under a black bridge, we seem hanging halfway up the side of the apartment buildings. There is water underneath us. People are talking again. The man beside me has gone away, after picking his teeth with a fountain pen. There are avenues in green and red and white lights running underneath us. There is a running in my toes. "I feel so proud of you, I feel so proud of you," a woman is telling someone behind me. I pretend it is me. The Pembroke girls have new faces on, sticking their busts out again as they push themselves into the arms of their coats. The girls are talking of fraternities and chanting upsilon upsilon. I stop now as this silver train has in Grand Central. It is very quiet. We are all lost in having found ourselves the city.

It is Monday, January 31, and there have no words down for three days, but I am back onto Beacon Hill. Friday evening in New York was wasted mostly in haunts like Lennie's Hideaway and Dirty Julius', but there was a picturesque hustler's haven on the edge of the Bowery, called Sammy's Follies. We stayed here until four in the morning, refusing the usual type of entreaties from the doorman, bar patrons, entertainers male and female, cigarette girl, camera girl, and the host. Do you want your pictures taken, boys, hi boys, want to buy me a little drink, want a bite to eat, boys, check your coats, cigarettes, drink up, boys, some real liquor this time, say boys, could you spare, looking, boys, and every time no, no thanks, but no, sorry no, no money, I am a poet, I starve, I freeze, I die. We were not told to come again, back to the great bosomed ladies with dollar bills inside their dresses who squeezed their bodies between tables. These were the entertainers, they were gay ninety, with boas and rasp voices and picture hats under mandolins. We sat in front of blown up photographs of Sammy from the Follies with Betty Hutton, Sammy with John Carroll, Sammy with Rocky Marciano, Sammy with Sophie, and Sammy again with Rocky, this time their faces were blown bigger. We left shortly after a group in gowns and tuxedos had been persuaded to climb the stage to have their pictures taken with each one of the cast, at a dollar a picture. They were not quite as drunk as we.   Oblivion by five.

At eleven, out on East End Avenue, out through the Carl Schurz park, out over the East River with the usual clouds and tugs and bridges, below the Gracie mansion guarded, out in New York alone. The dogs were in mufflers. A crosstown bus with regards to Broadway marquee boxoffices, and a ticket to a very careful American opera by Carlo-Menotti and suddenly eyes at the boxoffice eyes just another pair for the first time, away from the eyes to the Astor lobby, wall to wall rugs and people, the Astor bar, 20¢ of beer in a champagne glass, and sudden the eyes back, the same pair, mine to them for the first time, lips parting, small words over boxoffices and the state of American opera, wonderful state in the Astor bar, invitation to makebelieve, yes, why not, yes, but let's not take time out to eat, the deliberate unfolding of a twenty dollar bill, and it's yes, taxi taxi to E. 57th Street, into what one cannot believe buildings, as the eye drop door shut, up overall, water colors of Boston in the rain by Gerri Ricci and sculpted heads by Reg Butler, out again, into, up again, oils by Dufy and Utrillo and a maroon and grey room with a gilt mirror and a woman reading a grey paper in a pink slip by Vuillard; /above the little horns below a neon tower's time 1:39, it will never be 1:39 again here, on foam rubber and cigarettes in our hands touching for the first time in the empty gallery, Pierre Matisse one of his French woman singing through a bare hall laughing at us her audience, taxi again, bottled brown beer again, knees touching for the first time, Matinee Today the sign says on the sidewalk there's a matinee today and I'm going, with the furredcrowd and the giltliquidgrey hairs, yellow stub for the last row but close, into the overture and a small face beside me asking the singers, hair falling on my shoulder, curtain heavy velvet coming up, and the world begins, a drum then violins and the first clean voice, scratching of electric fingers on my back, and the voices come on, they carry Annina in with the red of Desideria's dress running from her hands, Desideria had bled a carnation for her hair, she unlocks the crucified with her kiss-and dances to make him make her die, still the clear voice of Annina, Sister Angela calls out to death over my head in the last row: Hold Back, O Death for still a little while, cold : Then come at last and make the night eternal for His eternal. The world ends. Makebelieve? Not yet. The usual in the Cameo by the Park, and hands again as usual under a table and shoulders touching in the taxi going through the highway of Central Park with the little gold thousand eyes watching that nothing possibly go wrong, how can it with god, good evening from the green doorman, and make believe made lavish on Madison Avenue with whiskey and cocacola and original oils and books (no walls) books, Salome, Dickens, Millay, Boccacio, Gatsby, Bryant, Pound, something to remember me by, The Cantos, the cantos mine, the entire Cantos mine, and lips touch for the first time in five hours, and an address on the white back of an envelope, 47 E. 87th, and for the last time in the yellow corridor, goodbye and taxi and home to them the ones Sammy's Follies who got out of bed at two in the after noon, with questions for me and no answers but excitement and small sleep, and then out to another velvet curtain going up on Saroyan, from the fifth row partial view right, waiting in the Time of Your Life for Gloria Vanderbilt, who runs whispers through the audience every time she moves in the barroom telling that all night she watches men die and that all they ask her for is a little warmth and some air, with music from negro hands, and saroyan good goodness for the time of our lives, live, and then death, because the fifth row is gone and I have people I am obligated to in Lennie's Hideaway and Dirty Julius' and the Minetta Tavern. Go to bed early

And not out at eleven the next morning, but I listen to lesbians talk while 1:39 chimes 24 hours later with lesbians, away from the foam of rubber and it was only our knuckles that touched the first time, finally out, still alone, but walking with the cold coming through my stockings attempting the glory of yesterday with the Greek and Roman remains, in the men's room, again with the Venus Genetrix fished from the Tiber and Dali and his cubed crucified Christ on a gold like a thousand lights cross, 13¢ for a bus on Fifth Avenue by the murdered Rubinstein's, "You'd never know there was a death there! Who, Helena? Who Artur?" Carnegie Hall but in the lobby, "No there's no way to get in now" and the music comes down the stairs as soft as making love, it is ice on my stockings and my scarf lost, yet the great Greta Garbo opens February 1st at the Normandie but today's January 30th even if there was no tax there wd not be enough. The library, the New York Library by bus and 13 more with vast plain halls and no shelves open, the theatre room's closed on Sundays, search for the family seal in the genealogical room snuck from because I can't read German, the men's room with the excess of men on the floor, catalogue of Pound and Wieners, everything under Pound no entry under Wieners, poetry and periodicals of, but more poetry in the big boy dressed in white copying fashion notes from Vogue, lost in marble halls barefeet on streets, the wrong bus to Riverside Drive and West End Avenue, and the ice on the thousand gold lights say that something has gone wrong, one doesn't know why walking from 86th to 81st past the Shurz park in the dark through little Germany in the night is real. Reality? Yes but at the end of Gracie Square the light from the window of the spiritual Stokowski with the beautiful hair and face and the voice that could never come higher than the heart's monotone in her make-believe home fast now. Sleep as often as you can on the way home, but home now and all the words are down.

Came home to Christianne from Providence and we slept in the same bed, she on top of the sheet and I under. Mr. Wieners will not be able to report work today, he's been detained in New York. The morning we spent under the monk with his horn to the sun on the spire of Church at Clarendon St. and Romeo and Juliet we decided to see & as the velvet curtain went up again and somehow again, things are ordered and precise and not wrong; they die not in chaos but remembered, she with her yellow head tilted against a bronze pole in a tomb with his head on her feet, and her face her mouth with the answers that this is not wrong, this is refuge, this is the momentary eternity, the dragon that has been carved to wind his tail in and out among men until they are no more. Her eyes like his black eyes touching mine for the first time.

Impression of the above; I am swept clean, empty, and do not dare to read it over again, for I write in the near dark, having begun in the light, and I shall not go back and make the blemishes unreal, as before. She paints my kitchen stove, and again I feel this is my happiness, my love, my strength, my food and sleep, I have found it, it coming through me, and I shall tell you ambitioners, I shall tell you hopefuls, go into it, do not give up, until the red rivers have run down your heart with joy, what I am saying is not what I want to say, I am only trying to say that there is something here will keep you strong, and sustained, you will find your hope here, I am not saying the words anymore, I am not telling you how I am sustained now, how I have never felt so fulfilled, so eager to be driven on and on like this forever, for here is my life, here I am possessed, I do not need another thing now, I do not need god, or wit or complement, but this shall go, and I do not care, for I have had it, and I want you triers to know that it can be had, It is nearly dark and only the white keys I can see.

Bob and I, I shall refer to him as V. throughout the rest of the journal, have been talking for the past two hours, and now he is my study, writing to Veronica the girl he is in love with, telling her for the first time in the many months that they have been together, that he loves her, even though last evening he told her goodbye. V. shall express himself tonight, he shall say of their perfect moments together, he shall talk of how their hands met over the program at the Gardner concerts, he shall tell her that he knows her problems, that he wants to help her, that he will give of himself to help her, he is going through some kind of pain, now, I know, I feel it, because he has never told her this before, he has been unable, and now because of our two hours tonight, he is able. This makes life worthy, he enobles the soul, to do what Bob and I have done tonight, I am so lucky, to have somehow found and opened myself to people. Rita and V. and god, I know somehow I am solace, I am heart to them, and they are heart to me, I want so much for them to find the expression and the peace that is all, as I sometimes have it, no matter how brief. The world is full of thousands, millions, who never find the fullness, who never live in the time of their life, who never have a time. I do, I have the time of my life in a hundred minutes of the day, even in the pain, and the burden. This happiness cannot last much longer, I am going too high, the air is too clean, I must go down, and the green office, and the thought of it have done it a little already. The People of the world are ripe, but one cannot get to know anyone, or like anyone, though they pretend themselves to do, as so many do, until they are in love with the people first. Christanne has gone back to Providence. As I wrote tonight the happiness and event of New York, she was sketching in the kitchen, and expressing it all inside of her, as I was doing in another room, the both of us filling white pieces of paper with new life, making them kitchen walls, and windows, and art galleries. How can I go on working? I shall quit tomorrow, but I cannot, I must pay the debts, I must have income, but there is so much of the world that I want to absorb, so many books that I must read, so much of time that I cannot let go by. But I MUST ACQUIRE DISCIPLINE. I must learn my art before it is too late and the running of love in my heart has gone to dust, and I will no longer feel. I know tonight that I have the fullness of heart, the fire, that can transmit to other people, and this is not always with me, and yet I must put it to sleep, because the bell will ring at 7:30 tomorrow morning, and I cannot ache all over, and my arms cannot be chained to the floor, as they were this morning, or else I will not go again, but this is why I hate my work, because it takes away the time, it puts one into channels that not only take away the actual working time, but also the time going and coming, the lunch hours, the dressing, the undressing, the cleaning of clothes, the thinking and mind work about the job after the job, the pettiness that is imposed upon the mind, the bug-men that one is forced to meet, and talk to, and worse of all, think about and feel sorry for.

Veronique is a German-born girl, not the American type, the college-girl type, but one that wears no loafers, and khaki pants, and her hair uncombed and her face washed clean. These things cannot be said about the American college girl. She has a face, and her mouth, although I cannot describe its shape and the little scars that are cut above it, is one that one remembers. Her face is not quite oval, and not quite square. Her hair is long brown, and her skin smooth and I imagine typically Teutonic.

She doubts the worth of Veronique, and she cannot dispel self-doubt. She wants to express herself, as all men do, but she has to express herself. She has said that she cannot sing, or dance, or play a musical instrument, or paint or write, although she does write and then destroys them. She is compelled to go out and attempt all of these things, she desperately wants to study in Vienna next year, she desperately wanted to be a ballet dancer, to have her arms and her body and her face before people, to be applauded, to be approved, as the old tree goes. This thing whatever it may be, will be her flag out before the world, he will probably make her a person in her father's eyes, V. has seen this. V. has great heart, he has the compassion that is a curse, that causes injustice of others to be injustice to him, not only the pity for the murdered ones, but for the murderers. This is the pain of the world that becomes his pain. This becomes constant apprisal of everything moving and living and dying in the world. He is in love with Veronica, and wants her to return his love, but tonight in the next room, he is not asking for a return, he is writing to tell her how much the perfect moments, their kiss, saved for the perfect instant, their hands over the musicale program, his arms over her shoulders turning the pages of the Spanish book, -- how not of this poor world --- all these meant. She has not fully known this, she does not know that she can bring something to his soul, she feels that there is no greatness in her, no capability for inspiration, she is little Ronny Alewin, and does not know that in his heart, she is the other world. She is the near-dawn fantasy in long brown hair, she is the searched for, she is Veronique, his greatness. I am tired now, and yet I want to go, I want to be here typing when he comes out, so he can know/ that I am the dedicated artist I pretend to be. I keep on pounding, I must release myself from the habit, not a very bad one, of typewriting. I felt elation for one instant then, for I felt that I writing something good, whatever one means by that, there is so much doubt, there is so much, that you cannot be sure of, I will stop now and go to Saroyan, no, I shall not stop now, I shall go on with my schedule, even though it does no good to me to sit here for three hours and write about nothing, a thousand words mean nothing if about nothing, if not new, but I do cleanse myself, I open myself for the pure to come in, I am burning away the dross that has accumulated throughout the bad years, and I believe that it will come, the great shafts of poetry will come, that is not dramatic, you there with your ever poisoning ones in your hands, that is poetry, great shafts, and that is all that life is. This shall be such an unreadable journal if anybody does ever read it. No one has, although I have read three lines or fifty words of it to Rita. And I have been tempted to read lines of it to Bob. I will not feel it can be read by anyone. I am too weary to go on anymore. End of Journal for Monday, January 31st/

Tuesday, the 1st of February
I went over the schedule today to compute how much I have accomplished, and of the two weeks and more of writing, I have completed my assignment only twice, but I shall not give up. I did not go to work today, either. I simply woke up this morning, aching again, and stumbled into the cold kitchen, locked the bell of the clock, and went back to bed again until ten. I then journeyed through the snow in my sneakers, through the dazzling gardens, they were never so covered with white, and spent two hours at the library looking through magazines, and pamphlets, and booklets that offer scholarships, fellowships and loans, and only succeeded at being depressed, because none of them applied to me, or I applied more accurately to none of them. god came, hurt, having looked over Boston for me, in my haunts, in the Bookclearing house and finally found me in the library. We had lunch together, and then I returned to the library to begin on my short story, concerning the man who rode the swans. For an hour and a half it came good, and then weariness, and

no strength. I came home over the hill in the snow, and had dinner, and R. came, and we went to the museum together in the subway. We heard a lecture on 18th century painting, the Flemish, French, and English schools, with none of them being able to create anything for me. The lecturer, Miss Dow, was a bitch, and she smirked over Marie Antoinette in her sheperdess costume, milking cows for two hours, but it was fine to be there with Rita. R. came home with me, and found Marie Conway, who has so enthused me about summer work camps in Europe, that I am sending my request for application through mails tomorrow. Somehow, I feel that I have had a satisfying day. J and B also were here, and J, over a beer in the double 7s informed me of his marriage in the coming September. J is one of my oldest friends, a boy sat beside me in my Freshman English and Latin and Greek classes, but he is a homosexual, and I do not think that his soon-to-be-wife is aware of this, and she is quite furiously in love with him, and I do not think that he intends to tell her of this scar in the eye, as Lorca has said. Europe with Marie Conway will be the most exhilarating experience that a human being could have within the boundaries of sanity, and yet after I have talked this over with god, it possibly be that I shall go, if they accept me and if all the details are made clear, and stringless. I shall Ezra Pound tonight, and mark up the copy to learn meter. I need the study of the craft of poetry, and I shall not get it while writing journals, and short stories about swans. I am not quite sure that there shall be a job for me tomorrow and it will mean back to the grand era of job-seeking which is more infuriating and degrading than any actual work on a job, by job, I mean the ones that I have always had to endure, mostly in the gloss and mechanics of the business world, the artificial, doomed, and stabilizing business world.

V. came out last night from the study after an hour and a half with four pages of writing. It was his passionate letter to Veronique, and he said the things that his immediate and impulsed heart said. He told his love, he told of the magic moments, of the concert moments, of the shoulders touching his knees, of their perfection together, and he asked that this should not end, that they must go on together to find these things again. He sealed the letter without re-reading it once. We are waiting.

Tonight with R. was dull, even though we walked through the snow in the gardens and read in a bright library together, and held hands, and each wore one of a pair of rotten leather gloves, but there was no magic. She does not bring enough to me, I am not trying because she does not ask me to try, and this is my weakness, but I must be careful with her, who has put herself close to me and I could step on her heart so easily, but she cannot just walk beside me, and smile at me, she must talk to me, and make me see the world that we are walking though as a new and somehow fascinating place, as all the people that I have been love with have done. They have made the world a special place, they have brought warmth and clearness, and yes, even purity to a somewhat shabby place. Every street with Rita has been a special street, and she has to make them this, or we are lost. She has to be enthused and enthusing, and I am weak. I need these things, as much I am able to give them.

End of entry for the new month February 1.

Entry for Wednesday, February 2nd.

Have finished two hours work on the story untitled, about the man and the swans. Am arguing with god about Europe, I am unable to type, how I want to get away from this, the door has shut. Tonight, Bilver and Hallelujah and Gilbert, and god --- all were here at one or another, chatting, asking, raising eyebrows, distracting, anything it seems, to keep me from the work that I sometimes want to be kept from. This journal is the only thing that I can get any peace from, all the others, the story, and the poetry, and the two unfinished first acts of my plays, only frustration, they only show me that I cannot persevere. This journal imposes no obligations on me, it is easy, the thoughts come down onto the paper as quickly as they come to my head, and I am free of them, but in the poetry and the story, I am afraid, I do not want to go back to them, I cannot say the things as I want to, I am hemmed in by how this line should be, and whether this word is right. If only I could become unconscious of the future audience and write as I am impelled to write, as I do now, that is the answer, but this does not matter as much, as the others. This does matter, but I cannot help it when I am writing here to let everything pour out, and not care about the form, and the meter, or the paragraph, or contractions. This is undisciplined and not good for me. I did not go to work today. They hailed me as the prodigal, and I have calculated that by March 30th, I shall have all my debts wiped off, and can begin saving as quickly and as much as possible for when I shall be free of the burden of the eight hours wasted.

I shall just keep on with this to fillup my three hour schedule. I should do poetry. I should be alone somewhere, and do nothing but poetry. But I am afraid of this. It is bitter here tonight and hard to walk away from room to another because of the cold. They say it is below zero, and all I have is two electric portable heaters for the four rooms, but it is enough. I am not really cold. One acts so much when he realizes he has an audience. People cannot understand how I can stand the cold, and so I pretend it is a labor, and that I shall be found some morning frozen in bed, but it is not so. In bed, I am perfectly comfortable, it is only in the mornings at 7:30 that I am near paralyzed. Otherwise like tonight, I am only a little damp.

I am thinking now of the excitement of those first early years in Boston. Actually they were not early years, only three ago, but I have changed since then, I do not go to the films anymore, I barely drink, the New York weekend was the exception, and yet when I am writing of it like this, all the desire for the black streets, and the lights with me under them comes back. Gilbert came up then, and I am impelled to write this down, he has invited us down for cocoa, and some old bed-chum of his shall be there, and it shall be bright and fun, and I will not have to think of this.

I read the Personae, and the memories of the black nights are going, and I shall leave them now, but they call me back, and I am not truly free of them, but not now as enslaved, as I once was. I am afraid that this now is my desire, at least for this season. No, I do not mean that, this is what I always wanted ever since that September day, when Millay was read to me in the back of the library, in a brown classroom. I wish now that I was a bright, silly, flying after fire, moth, and that I would be burned up soon.

End of entry for Wednesday, the 2nd. My three hours are down, but what does that matter. Poetry is as far from my soul, as if I was back in that Gothic room. Oh, send the warm rain soon, I must find the desire, the necessity again, or I shall be dried up like dust, what an image for a poet, and I must get away from this damned prose jag.

It is near midnight on Thursday, the 3rd. As bitter as yesterday, but tonight the damp has moved in. Have written nothing since today but these few lines, and what I could sneak in the mens room at work. I was tempted to quit today. Had to call god today for strength. Was told to have guts, guts, it takes guts to be a writer. I said, If I had any guts, I would walk out of this god-damn place and starve in the streets. This entry tonight shall be diary-like, with no singular prepositions, for speed only. Went to the library again today, and charged out again, Homer and the Iliad. Tomorrow night, I start translating with Jim Frates, from line 65 on. While at the library, saw the back-end of a book, and a familiar name, The auto-biography of William Carlos Williams. Picked it up, turned to the index, looked under Pound, and found at least twenty different page references. Turned to the largest, pp335-344, and began reading the chapter, entitled, Ezra Pound at St. Elizabeth's. It was fascinating to read of Pound's existence there. As Caroline Dunn said tonight, Just think what will come out after he is dead. It is becoming so literate he is dangerous, or something similar is how W.C.W. put it. The man is as sane as any of us, there is no question of that in anybody's mind. Was fascinated by the reading, and sat down, turned to the extravagant and cheap chapter heading, reading Ezra Pound and the F.B.I. At the end there was a catalogue of most of Williams' contemporaries. Every third name was dead. I wanted to copy it down, for it made me sad, to think that all these mad and enthusiastic, and rebel people (they were all rebels) were dead, or living in poverty, and not writing, or successful. Took the book home to list the lost ones for future use, and have become entranced and stimulated by many of the things I found there, while only looking for mention of Pound. This is the way that most of my knowledge has come about, by mistake. Found a mention of Charles Olson, who I have heard read at the Charles St. Meeting house here last summer, and who is connected with Cid Corman, Ferrini, Robert Creeley, and Williams himself. They all admire Pound very much, and seem to use him as their master. In Williams' book, there is an excerpt from an essay by Olson, called "Projective Verse" which has excited me, and seems a development of some of Pound, a true progression from Pound. It seems to be what Williams is doing in his own poetry. It shall be important to me, I somehow feel, once I look up the original, in Poetry:New York. I am also going to pay more strict and open attention to Origin, Corman's magazine, which seems to be flourishing without his editorship. Olson states, that a line should run according to a man's breathing, and this is determined by the emotion of the poem, or from his heart, and the syllables used in a poem, by a man's need. This is open verse, and mind-music, as Steve Jonas is constantly spouting. To think that a year ago, when I secretly considered to myself that I was a poet, I disregarded Origin as useless, was afraid of Ezra Pound, and Eliot, even though I had heard so much of them, but never understood what and for why they were doing their poetry. Now, I am beginning to see something, and shall use this knowledge for my own benefit and use. I will go back to poetry again, and this sort of thing is what I need, an admiration of men, an enthusiasm for men, whose whole lives have been devoted to its perfection. Not to poetry really, but to the poem. Mailed four letters to the Boston newspaper editors to have that hideous, revolving, blinking, pink-lit sign, taken down from Copley Square. It only means that I will have to look through all those letters to see if they print it, but I can do this for free at the library. I might go picket to get that hideous thing taken down. Have talked to the Dunns about it, and they are willing to picket with me, if it does not interfere with school and work, and I know God will, and maybe John Holmsey, and Marie, and Rita, and possibly a few others, if they see us beginning. The Dunns and I had an excited half hour together, talking about our future years in Europe, and my going there this summer, maybe, if I screw my courage to the sticking-place, also I myself grew mad talking about New York, and what on review has been my most hectic last few weeks. No one quite knows but V. how I acquired Pound's complete Cantos, but in reality, it is all very petty. With the Dunns, it was like the frenzied days of this summer past all over again. Screaming, shouting at the top of our voices. There might not be a Europe, by the time we get there, but there will be. Someone is making noises out in the hall, maybe for the typing so late, and fear, horrible fear, that is a basic weakness, had put me back with my nightmares again. But it is going, and I can say now that it is gone. With the Dunns, there is the youth and headlessness, and fire, that the great ones before us had, and which shall be found again in us, I truly believe. We are destined. They have opened the way for this destiny with their lives, at the expense of their security, and families, and all the horrible adjectives and nouns that seem so inadequate on paper but which become one's in the world. Since they have begun it for us, we cannot fail them.

Williams seems to be so timid and frightened much of the time, even though he puts on a mask of bravado and coarseness. Although a week with Ezra Pound was referred as an intensely literary week, he found it much too exhausting, and could not see how Pound stood it, as for himself, he was eager to go, gladly. I am not really able to leave, the last three pages have come out in such a rush, and all the thoughts of the three in the bookshop don't matter at all after this. One referred to Hemingway, "The archetype of the repressed homosexual, who made good" I wish I had the repartee for them, the "Eskimo," said that a writer's prime function was communication, and the third, the one with the hearing aid, and forty-year old face, said that he held his opinions, and found out that the critics always came around to them, it didn't matter to him what year they did, but he found that they always agreed with him sooner or later. And I, a prospective buyer in the first one's bookshop, did not say a word. I suppose that I did not want to put myself into a position that I was not sure I would come out victorious, I know that is the answer, but I thought of my former resolutions, not then consciously, but maybe sub, and I was impelled not to say anything, but like the writer, to take it out in my art. And yet, I say, someday, I will <u>speak</u> forth my views. I was afraid.

End of entry, the 3rd

Entry for Friday, the 4th.
Today or rather the last four hours of it, it is now near ten, have been most hectic.

Work was as boring, but today I did not fall asleep once, and so feel accustomed a bit to it. I did develop an argument though with one of the five bugmen, I was told that I was getting paid for taking orders, I did not have an adequate answer, as I seldom do, but still the entire thing is too petty to recount. Began my first Greek lesson of this year from six to nine, after leaving the green office at 5:30, I don't know why I am putting down these temporalities, I suppose to show the frenzy and rush and lack of food. Have progressed over the final 100 lines of the Iliad and am truly fascinated by Homer. I am going to learn the first book thoroughly. Had two separate beers at the double 7s, and came home to find Dana reading the Prophet of Kabran to Marie and Hallelujah, they were fascinated, that word again, and when I was not so impressed, as one can find the same thing in a philosophy book, they were shocked. Had lintel soup and sausage roll from supper which sausage I dropped on the floor, and then ate from Marie's hand. She can not go to Europe this summer, parental disapproval, she is only seventeen, but wildly wants to live in Boston next year with Rita, who is attending the senior prom of the grey Alma Mater, with a literary light, Joe Connare. I am very tired, and hope I shall be up for the Museum tomorrow at 11. There is no time left for us. Every hour is spent in waste at that job, and I cannot remove it from my mind, as the great barrier between me and my desire. But it shall soon be over, as another week has gone by, and more money earned, and more debts erased. After this tonight, I am writing to the Little Magazine, a very shoddy thing, called Pegasus, the Greenwich Village Poetry Magazine. I suppose I was attracted by the name, on all accounts, I sent them trash, my "Le Boheme," which is black painted against the pink living room wall of the Dunns, and another alliterative piece called Song for My Hersy, but very early, and not worth a cent, but I do like Le B. as it says me. They have gone to the lagoon at the Gardens for ice-skating. It is lovely there with the lamps from the paths, and the barogue bridge throwing all magnificent shadows on the ice. I am tired to go and it is only ten. I can remember when days ago, I was beginning my day at eight, and ending it at dawn. In the Heights this week, there was an article against Atheism which turned out to be the best proof for it yet published at Boston College, also a poor theatre review which I myself might have written, two years ago, and loved. I shall write the letter to Pegasus and cease. What is left for me, when I do not have the courage to write?

End of February 4th. Goddman them and myself, the bugmen and me.

Entry for Tuesday, the 8th.
There was no entry for yesterday, I have no excuse, only that I was spending time on my Greek, I copied the first twenty lines of the original into my notebook, and then the English underneath. This too, must be a short entry as it is past midnight. I meant to work on the poem tonight, a new one on this last weekend, but Bilver Plack came we began translating Rimbaud and talking of language, not really, as he was showing me how to roll my R's as in gread ink, or in Marie. I have much to tell, and shall come immediately home tomorrow, and spend the time, here writing. With Rita again tonight at the Museum, hearing a lecture on scenes from the Odyssey.

End of entry, and I feel unfaithful.

Beginning of entry for Wednesday, and again I have done nothing towards my writing. I have cleaned the apartment, taken a bath, arranged business matters, sent a letter off to B. V. and one to Norman Castle and another to Veronique Alewyn, and sent the essay off to Paul Gibbons on F. Scott Fitzgerald. Wrote to the Music Appreciation Society, to tell them why I have not paid my bill, sent the photographs back to Cyrus Durgin that I promised to return 365 days ago, paid a debt, and --- all this does not matter a damn because I did not work on my poem nor did I spend anytime here, writing of this past week-end which I want to do, as it was special. Rita was drunk and sang in the back seat of a car with the most wonderful emotional lilt and magic. we, v. god, she and I literally waltzed thru the halls of this house, singing "Vien, Vien, nu du allein" and we knew the moment beyond payment. This entry must end now for it is agony for me in the morning without some kind of eight hours. Although I never sleep it, I should add, I shall go in and read now, for maybe an half hours. Goodnight, for I feel slightly satisfied. At least the floors are clean and the dishes washed and those goddamns things should not mean any more than a cockroach in the bathtub. I am ordinary.

End of entry for February, the 9th.

And so I begin now what I think is the 45th or 47th page of my journal, and it is just like when you like a cigarette when waiting for a bus, it suddenly out of nowhere comes along, so people shall begin to invade me here. I shall go on writing forever, even though tonight I am drunk, and there is no one to console me, there is no one with my soul, god is inadequate, he doesn't even come back anymore, John Homsy is lost in the world, Marie is caught up in her own problem, and Rita wants to be an actress, and is asleep by now, and I am sitting here drunk, and alone, trying to make up for the last time, trying to set aside the strength for the coming week, but I shall not think about the coming week. I shall only think about the time of your life, the priceless moment when all is right, I frown when I put those words in for tonight now, this is not the time of my life, the lifeboats have been lost, and there is not even god's body around, to god for his bread and heart, that is what I shall put on my first book, if there is ever any, but I shall make a book, I shall write the poems for a book, if there is ever any, but I shall make a book, I shall write the poems for a book, I shall stand up before the crowd who comes for love and hope and some kind meaning to the world, but there is no use.

Everywhere men are chained to trees, everywhere the Alfredos and the Maries are crucified, Oh CHRIST, YOU are not the only one who has been nailed to a cross, Homer was, and someday I shall write and that shall be my cross, ah, but it is now, and I am insincere, for I have EMBRACED POETRY, AND THAT IS THE HEAVIEST OF ALL, even heavier than the weight of pansies, spelling out his name, on his grave, spelling out DAVID, spelling out the boy who is dead, the boy who has gone to feed the roses. I wish tonight I could stop writing, I wish the paper would run out, and I after it, but this is not the way I want,

There is so much pain, I must go to sleep on it, or I will not live, there have been so many wonderful things happening and they do not help. there is no one to turn to, except the end of the paper before me, and I see that end, and

Entry for Saturday the 12th

I am at John Homsy's sitting in an arbor above Wolleston harbor, and contented. There is a fire and Chopin again, and the sound of John below cooking chicken a la king, and all of these things do not matter, but I have written a poem today and that is why I am contented. I shall type it here. It is a good poem for it says what I am twisted about. But before, I shall tell about the gulls this afternoon. We drove by and I asked him if he would drive back to watch them. They were like white rocks in the sun. Some were diving completely into the pure blue water, and the others, hundreds of others were curled into hard balls in brown marsh weeds. I wanted to make them move and we touched the horn, and slowly like a piece of rough silk being unraveled, it was simply wave after wave of brown wings, row after row, as when little boys file out of church an aisle at a time. So these birds swept, seeming to start from left to right, one bird at a time, opening his wings, and as soon as they were opened the one next to him began up and on and on, hundreds filling the sky with brown and white and speckled triangular wings, a little frantic as we did not let up on the horn, and they became conditioned after a few moments, and although some of them went on further to nooks down the beach, the remainder settled down as they were, and all our horning would not put them back into the air. I shall now type up my poem, I am going to send it to Poetry along with one that has already been rejected by them, and when they are returned, I shall send to Civ/n? maybe or possibly to i.e., and I wish the people at Pegasus would return the two little pieces of junk that I sent to them. I asked them in a letter that I would like to hear from them soon, even if they only told me that they had burnt the poems for warmth, and that if they had not done so, that I would like them back so I could have them for warmth. We shall. I shall enclose a copy of the poem in this journal. Felt very bad the last few days. Marie in her agony, crying over and over again, what does it mean, John, what does the whole thing mean? And what can one answer, when they tie the little girls hands behind her back in two, and romance thwarted, girl, 15, and youth in suicide pact. me and Sue love each other two. god just kissed me and called me the suburban poet. Alfredo—enough of this.

Entry for Monday, the 14th. It is Saint Valentine's Day and I did not go to work until 1:30. I slept until quarter to twelve, and then called Mr. Castle and arranged for dinner tomorrow night. This was an invitation he extended last June and so on February 11, I accept. How do people stand me? Yesterday was hectic. No writing done. Was up and out before 11. Read the New York times. Bill Donaghue was here. Worked for an hour on my poetry. "The Lapwing for his fallen Maidenhair", this is the one I wrote and nearly finished Saturday and which truly made the whole weekend worthwhile. Left for the museum and stopped to watch Fr. Feeney and met Marie Conway and Joe Dunn and Jim Gillan, and god, and Edison Marshall. Feeney was his usual self screaming at Jim Gallin, calling him the Sheeney from the Jewish Advocate. Jim just smiled, blew smoke-rings, and constantly took pictures, but the priest always managed to hide behind someone, usually the little negro girl. Met Rita at the lecture, she is so faithful. Saw a bust of Homer which I have recognized and seen many times in all the Greek textbooks. Came back to the apartment Marie here and hysterical dancing, waltzing, imitating Mae West, Bill Donaghue still here and Chuck Kuell and Carole Senacle came over with her bleached hair, one of the cockroach society, J and B also were here and later Joe and Carolyn Dunn came in with Edison Marshall following them, and Dick Millard and Chuck Chivakos and Gil dropping in occasionally and then dashing out again. I read quite a bit of poetry. As I was reading Pound's translation of The "River Merchant's Wife: A Letter," Marie became very upset, and the second time I read it, I could not go as we were crying so loud. It was beautiful in a cruel way to see her and Poetry the cause of it. I would like to say so many things in this journal as it can never quite hold all the emotions and experiences that I want to put down. And as things are really beginning to be formulated, and new poems begun this will have to suffer, but as a poet I should put all the things I have to say into my poetry. Sunday evenings in the future will be the time for the meeting of the Poetry Group. It will meet here at six next week, and promises to have new faces, and new poems. As for the picket, Nick Deane is all in favor, and so is Steve Jonas from Garden Street, all rebels, and all willing to work hard for it. This is paradise. But I shall go now and write my "Lapwing and His fallen" . . . End of the poorest written entry yet.

Sat the 29th. 1955
I have neglected you journal. Tonight I am at John Homsey's. I am writing this because poetry will be inadequate but it is not and I shall describe what is going on downstairs in a poem. Oh music, sing to me of the music. Must come down and burn my fingers, tell me of the words for the music, for the singing of friends, the girl in the study with her shoulders

twitching under the candlelight, the fire making gold the hair of my beloved men and girls, keep me calm, Athene, muse, keep me classic, do not let me overflow in old words, but only sing through me of the fire and the then tubular notes being rushed out into the fire, Beauty is a white, flying stone thrown into a fire in front of us. Their voices are gold from the music and the air is gone. I could cease now but I have words to say, I want to put into words what only music has, the spirit that man has made, if only I had imagination. It is now when I am plunging down into myself to see what I can flush up and there is nothing coming that I know there is no greatness in me. There is nothing divine, but you are divine, Muse, and I ask you to come into me and create out of my emptiness the gold field of words. I can tell my images, gold black, fire, music, song, friends, lads, bodies, lips, mouth, face, soul, heart, this is what I have to give. I have no ivory sandaled woman with swift feet, I have no Othello, I have orgy of words to come out. No prayer for my mother but only other's words. If I could complete and pull out and up from within and down, if I could be emptied. Oh, muse, lament with me, lament with me, lament, alga, moi alga, nun moi alga,

Even milk must,
    turned in my mouth chalk

The piano and the hands, the piano's hands,
the gold fore, the gold girl, the head of the fore
head of the gold girl, fire, fire, fire masking gold,
and flesh, swishing under light on the piano.
Maree, Maree, the last stomp on the piano.
Entry for Tuesday the 22nd.
I have neglected the journal. But I have written quite steadily, slips of paper scribbled on in the john at work, at my desk, all these writings were journal like entries but today I feel I must write in the journal if only for discipline. Discipline is something

I am going to need now for the old things are crumbling. god is going. I can tell. Last night I told him why didn't he leave me, we were not in love any longer, I had nothing for him, I told him I wanted only one lover, and that putting my arms around him like he wanted me to do was no good at all as it didn't mean anything anymore, I told him I needed him two and half years ago, and that I was not the same person anymore, and so he left and I do not know if he will ever come back. John Homsey just knocked at the door and it is good for me to see him now. Rita is going too. She is too of the real world for me. I thrive on my make-believe. That is why I am at the bottom when I come from the theatre, that is why last night was bad because we had come from the Ballet, I saw Tamara Toumanova dance the Pas de Deux from Esmerelda, she was presented with bouquets of red roses, her dancer kissed her hand, she unwound a rose and gave it to him, she took her last call with the stem of a rose in her hand, the Russian escapees also danced to the gold and heavy sensuousness of Scherazade, and after it there was nothing left but to come out onto grey streets and come back into time, and wonder which was the best street to take to come home, what bar should we drink in, what time, what time, what time, as T. Williams said, in the theater there is no time, but here in the world there is nothing else, all our actions are meaningless in the face of time, while in the theater every gesture, every conversation has meaning, is pointed, has substance. In reality, nothing has. That is why I thrive on make-believe. I do not want to be told that queer is written all over my face, and have people laugh at me in bars, or have to pretend that one is glamorous and exciting, and that the world means something, I do not want to have to crawl into bed with someone, and wash my face, and shit. That is why I struck out at god last night, I want to destroy reality, I have the great temptation simply to run off to a movie, and cease thinking. "To cease upon the midnight with no pain" I wanted last night to sleep with no pain, and feel no morning.

John has talked to me for a while, and told me to go from the personal, forget myself and I suppose that is unreality as how many ever do. Today is Washington's Birthday and as he said holidays never seem quite real, they bring back the past, the old days when there was time off from school and different things came upon one. I do not know what but something happened on this day in my past which is a burden on me now. I turn to this not as an escape, but somehow as a reality. I shall talk about Rita. She does not come here anymore like at the beginning, she is at the ballet this afternoon with a neighborhood girl, watching Alice in Wonderland. When she first came here she was an Alice in wonderland, even though she pretended to have seen all this before. I knew she had not, but she learned about us too quick, all the mystery was unveiled before her young eyes too soon and now I feel there is nothing left to draw her back here again and again as before. There are many like her, and especially in this life. They come to a dream, because they have a dream inside them, and they find something which they is that dream come true. But they last only a week or a month and they are gone, there is no dream. The dream has to sweep floors like she must, and wear clothes, and oh stop moaning, in the morning of Washington's birthday. This is the end and I am only typing because there is nothing else for me to do. I have a bookshelf full with minds I want to know, and I do not want to know them now. I thought then that it could be I have embraced the wrong art, but it is not so, there has never been a doubt, no matter how dark the night becomes, or the poems few, this is my road, and it shall make all the difference. There is nothing else for me to do, true, but that is because I have made everything else in the world not worth doing. I have chosen this as the best and I shall never forsake it no matter if it leaves me or not. I am going to the movies, but I will come back to this, whether it is still here or not I will come back to it. I shall only write to fill up this page, and that is wrong, but it is writing and I am happy here and no where else. I went to the films with Bill Donaghue and Chuck Kuell, and saw Theodora Slave-Empress an Italian film with american language cleverly dubbed in. I went for escape and I did. If I only had money to get drunk. The Dunns are here and that helps but only partially. What am I looking for? Why the nervousness and inability to relax. Not once in my life have I relaxed. Music can relax me, but can I myself. Poetry cannot relax me, but reading can. I shall work on poetry. That is what I need to do . . . always.

End of entry for February, the 22nd, but not the end of February 22nd.

As Scarlet has said "Tomorrow will be better."

Entry for Wednesday the 23rd.
Today I quit the green office, sending them a note through the mail telling Mr. Stinson, the personnel manager that I was unable to continue my employment with the Lahey Clinic as my position was dead, and I was alive. I do not feel good about this as I have no money but one week's pay and the proverbial rent is due, and god I have left, for my independence, whatever that may be. I am going to meet him tonight for the last time, we are going to be frank and forthright, that is, he is, as I could never tell him of the depravity and desire and fulfillment that I have experienced. This was the only love affair that I have ever had, not to hold that body against me again, every inch of which I know, not to have the arms around me again, my arms are aching now to have those arms around me again. Never to have the mouth on mine, and the fluttering of the eye's lashes, the way they would flutter in the lamp. Not to have it when I wake up in the morning, or the mouth against mine again, or the arms. Where will I go to find those arms again. They will die somewhere else, and I will die without them around me, not to have the laughter anymore. There is none I want. But there is something else I want and if I do not have THIS LOVER, the poem, then I am worse off than with god. How confused, how heavy I have become thinking of the arms, and

the eyelashes in the light. And yet I give it up, for what? A dream, an ideal I will never conquer, a noun I will never wear. But I must go out for the noun and the dream and give up the reality of arms and mouth. I will give the lover to have the love. I once promised Dana that the last words on my mouth will be his name, and I remake that promise. DANA, DANA, DANA, shall be the last poem I write. I have smashed it all, and it is all my own smashing I am destroying myself for a dream, because that the dream can be true. And if it is, so? I have lost the reality then and dreams are lonely.

End of entry for the 23rd. At least, I will never have to see George Stevens again, or look across into the death deserving face of Betty Alden Perry.

Entry for Thursday, the 24th.
Yes, I shall never have to look into the death-deserving face of Betty Alden Perry. I wrote a poem about her. And I am happy. And I feel that today's entry shall be the last one that I shall write in the first person. I shall be the observer from this entry on. I say this because I have quickly re-read the first 50 pages, and it is filled with nothing but my intro-spection. I must forget myself. I did meet god last night, and the frankness and the forthrightness that I could never have told him, I did. That is because he uncovered to me his insides, and we are at the beginning again. The old exhilaration is back for me. I do not need now the brooding, the crying at night. Life ends. So what? All we need care about is that life may end too soon, before we have accomplished our dream. And so for this journal, I am going to fulfill the original plan. I am going to write of the world, not of myself in the world. I pity the world when and if they ever get this for their eyes. It is not good writing, and it shall be worse reading. They shall have to advance cautiously through its pages. But every word here has been genuine, there has been no put-on emotion. Yes, I am free of the green office. I am a writer, and I shall be poorer

than the writers then. It does not matter. It never has. All that matters is whether the writer has enough clean paper.

The new issue of Poetry has come, and it seems much inferior. Everywhere there is the measured line. There is no genuine line. They do not write from their hearts but from the measured line. Looked up the winter issue of the Hudson review as it has published Pounds Canto# 85. The thing was completely unintelligible, except for the line ½ observation & ½ texvn

½ research   & ½ texvn
½ training   & ½ texvn.

Entry for Friday the 24th, 1955.

Another day of freedom. I have been out into Boston since 8:05 this morning, actually doing nothing, but nonetheless free. I have never seen the sun come in so bright as it is now. I have missed so much, being shut away from the sun all of those days. I am very tired but cannot rest. But this is the end of self-journal even though it seems to be the thing I enjoy the most. Boston with the coming of the warmth reacts in the right way. The parks are dotted with governesses and little children playing on the paths, and poodles mouthing sticks in the flower gardens. There is a free and easy gait to the people even though their faces are still drawn and puckered, it must be because we are still in February. This is the cruelest month. The world is tired, or rather this New England world is tired of carrying winter on their backs. The first day of the real sun is hailed. People must quit jobs with the coming on of warmth. In front of the brick wall in the sun, with his pole on his shoulders, like Arthur to the wars, stands a window-cleaner. Porgy and Bess live again. Bess, you is my woman now, you is, you is, and you must laugh and dance for two instead of one. Oh, Bess, you is my woman now, no need for wrinkled brow. Somebody loves me, I wonder who, I wonder

Somebody loves me, I wonder who,
Who she can be worries me.
For every girl who passes by
I shout hey maybe
You were meant to be my loving baby.

This on first impulse seems to be good meter.

By the windows, the pigeons come between the sun and the wall and the wall is black for an instant. There is spring shouting in the hall. There is hammering on the streets. There is singing coming up to the windows, and the voices of Cassandra are far away. Cassandra is true, but will not be believed, and by not believed will be disproved. The hands that became dirty with the winter wind are being whitened now in the new sun, and to stroke them is like running the Charles river over them. They are becoming clean and smooth again in the spring water. The books put in dust are being thought of again, and they must come out, to be read and their magic will run with the magic of the spring. This is the time to learn new words, new worlds, and the wipe down and off the coated winter, inch by inch, covering after covering, taking off the old hair and skin, with ancient implements, slowly rubbing, picking off the hair and bad skin of winter.

End of entry for February 24, 1955, 2 years and 3 months at 11 O'clock tonight.

Entry for Sunday the 27th.
And will it always go on? Man or the best of man struggles for freedom, and when it is given, when all the barriers have been taken down, and the field opened at any price, one does not know what to do with it. He shall adopt ritual and much conversation and Greek sculpture and many friends to take away the freedom again. We are brought up slaves in other men's worlds, but hold our own inner world as the dream one, the one to be found someday over the rainbow. And the

rainbow is followed and over it is the world, and we step in, and look up and down its empty main, and we are lonely and bored. We go to sleep too long, we build the same houses that we left, we initiate the same people, or we turn back, for since the dream is found, there is nothing left.End of Entry for Sunday the 27th.

Entry for Monday, the 28 or Tuesday morning.
No poem today. It builds to an excellent ending but confused I feel to the reader. Wasted three hours today at least, but am doing something. Must, though I hate this subjective part, get a feeling of accomplishment each day or I cannot sleep. Wrote schedule tomorrow; but I am free and there shall never be a green office for me again. There shall never be George Stevens horrible voice or Betty Alden's horrible face. I can exist as I am existing now until the end of April I hope, and then what. I shall plan. The Lahey Check to March's rent, and the party proceeds shall pay April's rent and maybe if I am real phoney and invite more people to this charity ball, this rent-raising party, I shall have May's rent paid and not have to work until the middle of said month. Already I have invited nearly 150 people to this four-room apartment. Oh, Chaos, I court you.

     End of entry as I have said today in this new poem, After God has been Disproven.

Entry for Tuesday the 1st of March.
I have nothing to say but my own observations. I cannot give criticisms of anything but only subjective impressions. This might be worthwhile if what can be said is converted to solid and well-founded information, not simply bias and misguided truth. One fact accomplished since moving into Boston. I have almost divorced myself from the everyday crowd. I do not read the daily papers, the monthly magazines, except Poetry and the Atlantic, occasionally Time which cannot be relied upon, as they sacrifice the truth and objectivity to a slick phrase of

alliteration or a glittering adjective. I also read The New York Times weekly, only the theatre news and the book section. Also today I discovered the Hudson Review and feel that this is a quarterly that is superior. This winter issue featured the 85th Canto of Pound, a sequel to ChilderMass which I have never been familiar with before, a note on same by T.S. Eliot, excellent film reviews, good poetry, and a good quantity of it, and reviews of the most worthwhile books. I also read the contemporary Poetry magazines. I shall not read the Saturday treatment in its pages of Pound and his Pisan Cantos. True, the articles were written by Robert Hillyer, but were endorsed by the editors, the same editors that control it today. The article I remember was called Treason's Strange Fruit and they

Entry for Wednesday, the 2nd of March.
Today is a march day, with much sun, and headlines on every paper, Boy 14, Slays Sister 10, Asks Mother to Forgive Him, Says I Didn't Mean to Hurt Her, Fought all Day Over TV Programs. This is a march day in Boston and I suppose every other city in the world where the people call for the boys and girls to be brought forth to confess their sins. There are many photographs of a smiling, banged-hair cut girl, and the murderer, looking frightened and so fourteen, with his hair over his face, and his eyes coming out through. The Hudson Review this month, which I suppose has to sell for a dollar is excellent.

The street, Grove Street, is quiet in the sun, and in all the rooms on this side of the street, great bands of sun play through, showing the wine marks on the walls, the footsteps on the rugs, the unmade beds and oatmeal dishes in the tubs.

Lamont Library in Harvard features a Poetry room, called the Wood-Berry Poetry Room. It is stocked with all the necessary volumes of any poet that one would wish one could wish for. They have an extensive record collection, the finest that I have ever seen, they feature four long playing records of Ezra Pound, the voice of every contemporary poet, they possess a recording of W.D.H. Rouse reading ten lines of Homer's Iliad, the first ten lines in the voice and the tone and vocal pitch that we have been able to approximate was the Greek. Also

Later:
The dusk, the cold, is coming down now all over Boston. He could see them in the plaza by the Park Street subway, scrambling into the tunnels. Women with their heads down, walking fast, their arms against their breasts, the tall men from Milk Street with their Homburgs and their briefcases, walking fast, the Monitor folded under their arms, talking to other tall men, of what they were having for dinner tonight. They were running away from the dusk, away from the red light going down over the common behind the spires of the old churches, the insurance were walking through Copley Square, their handkerchiefs pulled tight, folded paper bags for tomorrow lunches in their coats, along Charles Street the nighttime Bohemians were beginning to take on their reality, they were thinking of what they could plan for tonight, they could call Lise, or Doris, there would always be a party, it didn't matter how tired they were, out from the department stores, the fat women like shopping bags full, the police on the miffle of the streets, the cars stalled, and now this is all over, there is a knock at my door, and this is all over, the night and the dusk because a fool came and knocked on my door are gone.

Later:
There can be no writing of the dusk now, it is in the middle of the early night and the streets are empty of the ones who were, it is shadows now that fill the streets, only the shadows are running along the sidewalks, sometimes an occasional step of man, or woman, or dog or cat, but they are the shadow ones too, they are as hurried as the early ones, except these might be drunk or running off to more glamorous rendezvous than the men and women of Milk Street. Bah!

Entry for Thursday, March 3rd.

In fifty-five minutes of sleep, from 10:20 until 11:15 these are the following dreams I had. All very real, all in color, very definite colors, I can remember the blues and the rich velvet of cushions inlaid, the blond mahogany of furniture, the evergreen of Christmas trees, the rose in a woman's hat, she was a negro, the pale cream of a girl's slip. I shall begin with the second dream. I had gone to visit my parents in their home, I have taken my typewriter with me, my mother and father have just got home from visiting relatives and in the house is my sister Marion, my small nephew Richard, age 3, my uncle Charles, my mother who is intoxicated slightly, and other members of my family, my aunt Christine, except now she is very fat and dressed in a flowered housecoat, my aunt Ella, my old aunt, Ellen, I am in the house, and I find it is not the old family house but another, it is very crowded with furniture which I think is very cheap, until I look at it closely and then it seems to be rich mahoganys, and fine maples, but it crowds everything in the house and none of the sets seem to match any of the others, although the sets themselves are perfect. My mother is very excited, and in old clothes, except I know she has just got home because there is a navy blue straw hat on the back of her head, in every room there are Christmas trees, of different shapes, some dark green and heavily ornamented, others lighter green and on tables, behind one in front of the fireplace, is a great candlelabra of gold, it is very thin and can hardly be seen behind the Christmas trees, I hate the new house, and I tell my mother she should never have bought

She does not like it either, and I feel guilty because I feel by my leaving home, I have forced them into buying this ghastley house, filled with all kinds of furniture, which I remember my mother is always knocking over or bumping up against, my small nephew Richard is pounding on my typewriter and I make him promise that he will not play with it any more, I can remember looking out of the window and seeing people in the street, but the street I see is the one below my apartment windows in Boston, there are people in the street, two or three, they are young, and they are going into the house directly across from my living room, I look into the building and see on the second or third floor all the curtains up, and the room behind the window is completely visible. All the furniture has been taken out, and the walls have been lined with tens of full rich heavily embroidered grey and maroon silk cushions for the guests, I sense there is a party going on.

It is a very bright and gold-appearing room, I am delighted and amazed at, I call out, "Marion come here quick, look at this, what a wonderful idea". Just as my sister gets to the window, also another boy, called Omer which I know from the 77's, gets there, before they have a chance to see what I have seen, the lights go out, and all that can be seen there is a girl getting dressed with the help of another girl, we can see her silhouette in different fragmentary poses, it seems she is trying on some kind of party costume, with red letters on the front. I do not know and I am embarrassed that they should think I called them to the window to see this rather than the beautiful room, but Omer laughs, and says, Thank You, as he goes back, I look at my typewriter, and I see many of its keys are missing, I say, "Marion, look what someone has done to my typewriter, all the numbers are one from the top row, but the 7 or 6, and many of the letters of the alphabet are missing, especially from the left hand corner. I look around to see who could have done it, and Richard is playing under the window, and I pull him over, and I can tell by his face that he has done it, and he will not say he is sorry, I say, Do you think that you should have done this when I asked you not to, I am very patient and kind, but he will not say that he is sorry, and I speak to his mother, Mary, but it does not seem to bother her that Richard has ruined my typewriter. I am not sure now whether this section I am going to describe came before the window episode or it happens as I am getting ready to leave, I have only stayed a short time, I tell mother that I am going, I follow the ritual I always do, kissing her soundly, and ask her if the relatives know I live in Boston, she says no, "And don't you dare tell, I never have," and she says something ambiguous and witty which I cannot remember, I take a book under my arm and I say goodbye, I remember my aunt Christine running down a hallway, a fat silhouette, there are many doors in the short corridor and they seem open, she is laughing because my aunt Ellen has said something to the effect that once she finishes her examinations she thinks she will go to college, I shout goodbye to my father who is upstairs, and who I cannot remember seeing while I was there, I look upstairs, and someone mentions what a wonderful curved and graceful staircase it is, but as all through this part of the dream, I am unhappy and see the broken wood in the stairs and do not find it pretty at all, I ask someone about if they have their Christmas trees up already and they say no, Christmas Trees? Why it's Easter. It seems the people my parents bought the house from have never taken down the decorations which are everywhere, and yet the last memory I have of my mother is being under the Christmas trees, still drunk, stepping on ornaments, and saying, Now that's done, all I have to do now is, and I can see Dana or feel Dana there, looking at her, and saying it runs in the family, but I think, "she's happy, because when I am like that figuring, now that's done, all I have to do" etc. etc. I am happy. I do not remember going out, but I am now on Mt. Vernon or Pinckney Street in the daytime, and all the window ledges which are close to the street are filled with books, it is quiet and the only people who are there are young boys like those seen at the Boston Public Library and they are pushing their book carts around, distributing and collecting books as I have seen them do many times at the Library. Richard is there and he is just as unconcerned as ever, but when I look at him closer (doing this) I ask him, "Richard, how old are you now" and he says 11 and a half, which I because all the years have gone by and I have not done anything with them, and I think, "well, eleven and a half isn't too bad, he can still learn understanding and sympathy, and I thought of how I was at 11, and I remembered that I was cruel and as inconsiderate as he is now, and I thought he will change, because I felt I had, and while I was talking or thinking this, I was twisting one of the large carts they use to carry books, and on the red pavement in the sun, all the heavy old books kept dropping out, and the cart never seemed to be under my control, I was unhappy about the poor way Richard had turned out, and I can remember looking at him, taking down books from people's windows, the windows were only three feet from the street, how he must have heard his mother and father fighting, and this has made him unhappy, but then I thought of how carefully his mother had brought him up, but then I thought he might have overheard their disputes without them knowing it. His age was the most striking memory of the episode as he was three and looked three, and yet on Pinckney Street in the sun, I could see a faint moustache, and he was tall and very thin, dressed in a blue gabardine jacket as before. I was now in a park and there were animals, I am leaving the park, supposedly coming home, and a tiny horse was running along the path, its belly nearly touching the ground, with a great bushy tail, it was nearly blonde, and very fast behind it was its mother, a disjointed and comparatively small mare as horses go. She was trying to catch her runaway, I identified him for some reason as her son, but he was going fast, yet I had no doubt that she would catch him, although it was nearing the very busy Streets, it could be the upper part of Tremont street near the State, with the paths that run parallel to this street the scene, except they were much narrower, and concrete and winding, they were nearly out of sight, but I saw her gaining and she nearly put her mouth on his tail, when a average size horse, also brown and very healthy and well-developed (only his head was visible) put his mouth into the little one's head, just as his mother put her mouth into his tail.

I could hear them carrying him back, and he was crying like a baby being tormented. They were not horse sounds but the sound of a baby crying. I walked on and I walked past a colly who I figured took part in the rescue, but I walked a safe distance from and out into the street, even though I could sense that the cars were very close and the fear of the cars running behind me, crept up my back. Another dog, fat like a bull dog was on the sidewalk so I couldn't get back, and then there were many cars along the side of the road with dogs leaning out of their windows forcing me further into the street, but I couldn't go further as I knew I would be hit so I tried to be brave and walk past the dogs who were chained but their chains were long and loose and could easily reach me, they just looked with fierce faces, and once or twice, a dog in the background would growl. There were not more than six cars, but outside the last ones were their owners, all girls, all looking alike, tall with black short hair, thin, with pretty faces, but as fierce and evil as their dogs, they were also all dressed it seemed in blue, and smoking cigarettes, with their arms raised all staring at me, as I walked along, I shouted out vehemently, "I hate dogs". I got to the top of the road, it was inclined street, similar to others I have been on, and there were many people here, waiting to cross the intersection except fire engines began to sound, and they were, It seemed coming towards this crowd, there was a woman in front of me, and I pulled her back by her coat strap, very hard, but I thought doing her service, no engines went by, and I said I'm sorry I pulled you back that way, she said "That's all right, you can't help doing these things," I thought she meant when you get panicky. It seemed we understood each other. She had a white straw hat, very silly perched on the top of her head, like the one I saw in Sabiens, which I thought was silly, except this was whiter and had a large red rose on the top of it, while the one in Sabiens was orange. I smiled at the woman, she was negro and fat, and nodding. Voices in the hall woke me, but colorful or frightening or confused or desperate or guilty than the one I am in now. Except I have the peace here of writing and the great purgation and blessing that it brings with it.

the dream world I left is not any less

The dream I have omitted is a shorter one and the first, and it deals with a short scene I have seen in a film or dreamt about before. I walk into a small room. Vivian Blaine is there singing some kind of a Mexican number in a gray sequined evening gown with a long chiffon futa? scarf in her hands. She is tall with long blonde hair, excellent figure, and her voice is awful. The instant I heard this woman singing this morning, I knew that I had heard her before, and that I thought, why, she can't do that again, she already sang that song. somehow I was in the floor show, and with her, except the timing was bad and we were left waiting on stage for the negro ass't. to come from the wings, he did, but still we were left on stage, Miss Blaine disappeared, and as I tried to get up from my squatting position, which one of the routines in the show had ended on, the negro held my arm by the elbow and wouldn't let me rise. The only remarkable thing is that I suggested that I read my poetry since there had been some delay. Someone agreed, and said yes, let John read his poetry, but no one seemed to pay any attention, and the remaining audience consisted of some small petty friends from my home town, who were talking about the party I am going to give this Saturday night. One got up to leave and I asked him to bring his date to the party, but he was non-committal and surly, shutting the door before I finished. I think that this is how I came home to my parents, because these people from my native town were in, the first part of my dream. Well, it is recorded and for the main purpose of showing you how insane 55 minutes of existence came be. And the added irony is that it has taken me over 70 minutes to transpose it to you, in this form.

Tuesday, March 8th, 1955

Since I have not been able to get out of bed until 1:00 in the afternoon, and have wasted the remainder of the day in worthless pursuits, it has been necessary for me to bring my typewriter to the side of my bed, so that I may write here in bed as Proust did, a fact I learned from a Lauren Bacall movie. And I am very uncomfortable, but I am writing the first words since last Thursday, whatever they may be worth. It has been a most disconcerting and unreal few days. I shall begin with Friday evening. I returned from my Greek lesson, line 175 in the first book of the Iliad, and I was. my whole reality or waking time was taken up with thoughts of Saturday evening's party. David Fowler and Marie Kaufman from Providence and the Rhode Island School of Design were in the living room with Dana and Marie Conway, and two quarts of gin. David made me a toasted martini, but as he was burning the lemon oil the glass smashed in his hands, and emptied the gin and Molly Pratt vermouth onto me, a fact which I shd. have taken as an omen for the past few nights. A harbinger of confusion. This is bad writing, unfortunately, as what I am going to write about is of the richest experience. They were fascinated with Beacon Hill, mad people that they are [. . .] I took them to the sevens, which fascinated them. Dana stayed alone at the apartment drinking martinis, as he was weighted with a cold. The sevens were only beginning to be crowded with the Hill characters, and there seemed to be an unusual lack of tourists from across the river, which has always acted upon the natives to do wilder and less inhibited forms of exhibition. Marie and David seemed impressed. David circulated. Marie drank wine, and also circulated her eyes, Marie Conway watched and left after an hour, and a boy called John Homsey joined our table. This was the beginning and the crowd increased. Exuberance rang loud. At one booth, there was a game of spin the bottle, with men and women, husbands and wives participating, no holds between any of the sexes. A short physical description of sevens should here be included. It is not any more than 24 feet wide at its roomiest point, and that includes bar and bartending space. It is at least 100 feet long, and when a crowd enters and is formed, there is nothing but a continual shoving and excusing through the bar. This naturally precipitates many fights. My job for the previous five days had been to canvass the bar at 9, 11:30 and 12:30 every evening to invite fresh new faces to my party, where I hoped I would make a $100.00. so that it would not be necessary for me to work any longer, at a job comparable to the Lahey Clinic. I was chatting, joining in spin the bottle, and making a complete bohemian of myself, dropping plates on the floor, having two bottles of beer emptied over my forehead, etc. etc. when I felt someone pick me up and carry me in their arms back to my booth and I remember shouting "Put me down, put me down." I was not drunk and I was glad to relax and wait for Marie Kaufmann who had left with a man just returned from Mallorca, with the promise that she would return at 12:45. I waited. A thin man in grey flannels, young, and my build walked past our booth and shouted "Put me down, put me down" at me. He went to the men's room, and returned again saying to me, "Put me down, put me down". We had foolish words together, I remember going down like a feather to the floor, I got up, Dana, Good Old Dana was there, more words again followed, and I remember hanging onto the white shirt around the laddie's chest, and ripping off a complete rectangular square, into which I blew my bloodie nose, and handed it back to him. The barroom, 24 feet wide, was in an uproar. Marie had entered the front, remembers seeing Dave Fowler, like an old log in the backwash, being carried to the front of the bar away from we were in conflict. I remember turning around and seeing the place in complete chaos. Young fellows were standing on top of tables and booths and bar shouting and looking towards our corner of the ring. There was great empty space surrounding us. The bartenders were around, rushing shouting, hurtling us into our coats, barring us for life. Bystanders were taking sides. Lise, the party-organizer of Beacon Hill looked at me, with great eyes. We were thrown out, into the cold back to the martinis. We had then Dana, John Homsey, Earle Pilgrim, silversmith, painter, and proud, Marie Kaufmann, John from Mallorca, Dana and myself. We came to the apartment, David, Marie, and Earle, with John Homsey's oils and brushes, and began painting and portraiting my white living room wall. They lasted until five in the morning, and my wall was nothing but giant blobs of oil, applied mostly with bad brushes, muddy turpentine, and drunken elbows, fingers, and palms. On one wall, since I was their only model, are two portraits of me, which even I did not recognize the next afternoon. The next day was hung in oblivion, but at six thirty, after having run through the knee, or more accurately mid-calf deep snow of Boston Common, and Gardens, to buy 100 paper cups, the party of this year on Beacon Hill began. Everyone was asked to donate a $1.00 bill as it was a rent-raising party. I had asked all opposites, from female impersonators, to poets, to small town garage mechanics, to clerks, back to painters and ballet dancers, and hairdressers, male ones. Dana was stationed outside the hall door, asking the $1.00. Marie was with him, marking inside of each person's wrist, at seven they began coming, at 10:30 there were over a hundred people in my four rooms, and someone turned down the main switch, casting the entire house in black. There were twenty-one gallons of cheap wine, and complete bedlam. I was circulating with a silver urn, shouting Grecian adjectives about myself, an Italian named Alfredo was on a stool in the middle of the living room singing Wein, Wein, nur du allein, and everywhere there were people. At eleven o'clock Dana had slightly over $104.00 in his pockets, and the police were on the stairs screaming that everyone must leave. The lights had come on again and here the incidents began. Lise's great eyes were red with anger, she would soothe the police, I was angry, multitudes had paid, and now they were being turned out at 11 o'clock, only 12 gallons having been drunk. Most left quietly as I promised them that the door would be open to them for the rest of the night. The police left. The knocks began again. Is John home, where's the party, I have some liquor, is this 38 Grove, Is John there, and then darkness again. As soon as the police had left, the evil hand at the switch, I suspect the man on the first floor, turned the house of lights into blackness. For the next half hour, there was nothing but knocking on the door, and then shrilly, the voice I heard going by the booth, the little elf who puts people's feet on the gas instead of the brake was outside the door, and then a friendly voice, and then fighting in the hall, and the friendly voice calling, Help me, Help me John, he's choking me, and as reaction, we rushed into the hall, and then there was the beating of me hands on his flesh, there was nothing but our voices shouting for his blood, his body hunched over, his face turned away, and we brought him to the top of the stairs and let him go. I could hear a little girl crying at the bottom of the stairs. The lights came up again, Dana had blood on his arms, the friendly voice was gone. The shrill voice was gone, and five policemen were in my kitchen, only different ones this time. Wine was running on my kitchen floor, all the windows were open, in the windows across the street were tens of little faces peering out from respectability. I had achieved what I set out to do. They questioned, they evicted the rest, they shone their lights in every room, they cursed, wine was on every wall, my books were down. Four of them rode with me in the car into the station. Another dream was coming true, I was going to spend the night behind bars, and to top it all off, there was a 104.00 hidden in a coat in the closet. I thanked the officer who rode with me in the wagon, I told him he was a sadist, they referred to me as the party man, because when they asked me what I did for a living, I answered them that I gave parties for a living. They took off my belt, they left me with cigarettes and no matches, they marched down a long corridor under yellow lights, and put me behind bars, thick and black, and the steam heat took breath away. The steam heat was up my nose, it was in my throat when I walked up a grey street of melting snow the next morning, it was in the sound of voices all night long, shouting water, Water, how about a glass of water, I want water, it was in the doughnut they put on the bars of the cage the next morning for breakfast, it was in the urinals that flushed dirtier than they were before, it was in the voice telling Frankie that he was going to tell the judge that he would leave for Bangor the next morning if the judge would let him go, it was in the face of a man the next morning who when they called the name Harrigan stepped up and said Fahey, although I might have given Harrigan as my name last night. It was steam heat that screamed through the walls when ever a prisoner pushed the button over his urinal and a great saahwhoom thundered into every dirty, wall-cartooned cell, I slept on a board, and I did not think of a word but $104.00 and freedom, not freedom from jail, but freedom, to punch my hands against a typewriter for as many hours as I wanted up to at least April 20th. And thus I sit here in bed under silk covers, with the base of my back aching, and the top of my head aching, happy because I will never have to look into the face of Betty Alden Perry again, and this is the first chapter.

End of entry for Wednesday, or Tuesday, March 8th.

Entry for Thursday, the 10th.
I am not sure that this journal is a good idea, despite the fact that it has given me an outlet, I have not saved anything for the writing that I want to do. I read Pound, against him what can one do? If this journal were only a sideline, something that I turned to for relaxation, I would be satisfied, but it is something I turn to for expression, and that is not good.

I was very drunk last night, I was in a bar on the lower end of Washington Street in downtown Boston. I have had much to run away from, I suppose, and I did not have much money to do it with, so I smiled at hideous little people and let them buy me drinks. It is a very cheap bar, a boy they call Josie McGrath was there, and he shouted out that he was afraid to go home and shave himself because he would cut his throat. It is bottom of the barrel hangout, as a customer said, it is nowhere, and the people there have gone nowhere, and are coming from nowhere. I was pulverized, we acted up vile, I did not go out this afternoon until three or more accurately four-fifteen, and it was twenty-four exactly from when I had gone out the day before, and I had accomplished nothing, I walked the same street, I had the same clothes on except for a different pair of shorts but today, I did not have to run into a movie, today I walked along the Charles and waited for the sunset. There was none. The sun was sucked down behind great grey clouds, and left with only tiny tints on the edges of the sky.

Entry for Friday, the 11th.

By the water again today, the grey water, with the sun sprinkling goldust on the waves, and the world in grey mist around me, and the blow blowing our papers out to the harbor, under the bridge where Longfellow wrote so movingly, that they named the bridge after him; and the streets of my city loud with the moving of a thousand cars whose drivers do not know that all about them the world, the big-breasted, loose-moraled world is going to sleep again alone, only the road in front of them, their eyes only on number plates, maroon dirty dull maroon number plates, and the crash of other cars will not stop them, the red light of the sun will not stop them, and goldust on the water will not stop, the goddess with gleaming eyes will not stop them, not the perversion of the sun being sucked behind a cloud will not stop them, not the propellers of a duck will not stop, nor the green bronze plates of the old houses with their vanished gardens running out to sea will not stop them. They go on to Uncle Miltie and the Bishop, the Bishop shouting shit overall the antennae, and Bishop Shitean says, and Fulton says, to all the young girls, their small bosoms quivering under parochial school uniforms, telling them that we are wrong, we are the night prowlers to be avoided, the degenerates whose faces every girl in this park knows, what the hell are these girls doing out in our park with their uniforms pulled off their shoulders, and their little shoulders white in the night, their painted shoulders luminous under the far glare of the neon from Tremont Street and over them, the others are the multitudinous sparrows, fighting for a place of sleep in the pillars of the old Majestic, and the old ladies go home with their cupcakes in their cartons unaware that death duels are being fought above the Majestic more intense than anything ever put on inside. The air is cloudy with the sparrow and above the whirr of the thousand Chevrolets beats the fighting of a thousand mega, muria, squishy if squeezed sparrows. On the tops of every tall tree in the Boston Common are the buds of black, they appear so, sparrows. I cannot hear the world with the sparrows, and the cupcake ladies whisper, spring is here, and I smile it's wonderful, wonderful at the 300 carnations, 25¢ a bud, that stand on Charles Street in early March, there are only a few tulips but they are full and smell less than the carnations, but are brighter, and the street, West Cedar, is full of Daffodils, Daffodils, 25¢ for two. a quarter for two dozen, and Earle, in his shabby, paranoia, drinking Zinfandel from a milk-bottle because he would rather drink from a milk bottle until he can afford Regency Goblets, he only wants six, but he shall drink from a milk-bottle until then, and I drink, his awed guestdrink from a peanut-butter jar, says, It's like London, even though I think he does not know what London's like. Yes, back to the water, with my head against a stone pediment, watching waves, wanting to go in and under, and when the wind blows me down, holding onto pediment for survival. Because it is necessary tomorrow night for me to see the sun being sucked behind a cloud.

Entry for Saturday, the 12th.

At five-fifty-five on the 12th day of the 3rd month of the 55th year of the 20th century, what has been put up against oblivion?

What have we built?

What has any of man built?

We can do no more than peck off momentary eternities, chisel them, knife off the baroque, sprinkle with holy water and send into The Great Magnet that does not so much draw to itself but send off, to zenith and nadir, the complete fragments for eternity, or as much of eternity as we are given, not us, but Us, the ones who left bulls on the walls, temples to Zeus.

Quote from James Hilton's *Lost Horizon*

"There is a reason, and a very definite one indeed. It is the whole reason for this colony of chance-sought strangers living beyond their years. We do not follow an idle experiment, a mere whimsy. We have a dream and a vision. It is a vision that first appeared to old Perrault when he lay dying in this room in the year 1789. He looked back then on his long life . . . and it seemed to him that all the loveliest things were transient and perishable and that war, lust, and brutality might some day crush them until there were no more left in the world. He remembered sights he had seen with his own eyes, and with his mind he pictured others; he saw the nations strengthening, not in wisdom, but in vulgar passions and the will to destroy; he saw their machine power multiplying until a single-weaponed man might have matched a whole army of the Grand Monarque. And he perceived that when they had filled the land and sea with ruin, they would take to the air . . . He foresaw a time when men, exultant in the technique of homicide, would rage so hotly over the world that every precious thing would be in danger, every book and picture and picture and harmony, every treasure garnered through two millenniums, the small, the delicate, the defenseless---all would be lost like the lost books of Livy, or wrecked as the English wrecked the Summer Palace in Pekin."

(the above is a monologue by the High Lama of Shangri-La, not included in the preface, but worthy of inclusion)

(Now a dialogue between the High Lama and Conway, the searcher)

"I share your opinion of that." (The above.)

"Of course. But what are the opinions of reasonable men against iron and steel? Believe me, that vision of old Perrault will come true. And that, my son, is why I am here, and why you are here, and why we may pray to out-live the doom that gathers around on every side.""To outlive it?""There is a chance, It will all come to pass before you are as old as I am.""And you think that Shangri-La will escape?""Perhaps. We may expect no mercy, but we faintly hope for neglect. Here we shall stay with our books and our music and our meditations, conserving the frail elegancies of a dying age, and seeking such wisdom as men will need when their passions are all spent. We have a heritage to cherish and bequeath."This is all that I care to record from the actual work, but here should be the inclusion of the remarks from Mr. Hilton's preface to same book, later edition.

"When 'Lost Horizon' first appeared three years ago, its message of the peril of war to all that we mean by the word 'civilization' was considered topical.   (storm)

"It will be such a one as the world has not seen before. There will be no safety by arms, no help from authority, no answer in science. It will rage till every flower of culture is trampled, and all human things are leveled in a vast chaos."Conway answered: . . . "A similar crash came once before, and there were the Dark Ages lasting five hundred years.""The parallel is not quite exact. For those Dark Ages were not really so very dark—they were full of flickering lanterns, and even if the light had gone out of Europe altogether, there were other rays, literally from

China to Peru, at which it could have been rekindled. But the Dark Ages that are to come will cover the whole world in a single pall; there will be neither escape nor sanctuary, save such as too secret to be found or too humble to be noticed."

How much happier one would be to dismiss all this as thoroughly out-of-date than to admit, as one must that in 1936 it has become more terrifyingly up-to-date than ever!London, August 4, 1936

Transcribed in 1955, when the world is on the edge of a hydrogen chaos.

The minutes between Saturday, 12th and Sunday the 13th.
The life of the city at this hour has dragged sleep out, has pulled sleep out of my bedroom. In the room around me, in the lives around me they are breaking glasses, cracked voices are going up the airshafts, and through the far streets are the blare of horns. Over in extinguishing neon area, the girls are streaming from the bars, walking arm in arm in front of waiting headlights, soon they will come under these windows, their voices light with whiskey sodas and gin fizzes, talking to the sailors they meet out of open windows. Downtown, on the corners are the other lonelies, as Auden calls, waiting but not for light girls, for the other lonelies they can take home to bed. In Bickfords, the young queens are parading through the eyes, carrying coffee they will not drink; on top of the sidewalks of The Boston Gardens will be the feet of pacing men, young feet going back and forth over the same cement, stepping into cars, pressing down on the toes of other feet; this is the hour of the tryst; out of the hotels the bright women are coming, champagne glasses or beer glasses still in their hands; the lobbies will be full of men and women going up in elevators to twin beds, only one of em mussed, as the song calls, it cannot be told how the streets are now, how full they are with warm rushing people, how fast everyone is walking, how light over

the old sidewalks the heels are falling, these are sidewalks that wait all week for Saturday night, that take all week the shop girls, and the business men, and the housewives with cupcakes and argyle socks, who wait for the weekend when the shopgirls will be temptresses, and the housewives shall be in bed. The barmen are counting their tips, the hatcheck girls are meeting busboys in the kitchens, the negroes on the Corner of Massachusetts Avenue and Tremont Street are waiting, waiting for I have never seen what, but their waiting is more exciting than the confusion of the bars and poolparlors they lean against, girls are being given ecstasies in the back seats of cars all over Boston, the city is alive with orgasms, and yet under it all is Monday morning waiting more insistently than death, with alarm clocks, and this is the reason for tonight, this is why the frenzy, this is why there is breaking of glasses in the rooms around me, the horns are blaring out against Monday morning, and 8:30 time clocks, and insurance reports and that first coffee break, and the asking eyes of the fellow workers what did you do Saturday night, and they are doing it now, the great city too is doing it now in protest against Monday

gloomy Sunday, as Miss Holliday sings,

Thursday night, Saint Patrick's night, March 17th.
I write this out here. Rita has gone, as it probably obvious as there has been no mention of her for so many weeks. I thought I needed no one, I thought I could live without the gods, without the little Ritas and their dreams and makebelieves. She left, not that she ever really came to me, I never actually kissed her as I might have, but it has been nearly two weeks since I have seen her, and it was two weeks before this that I had last seen her. The dream she had of me has been smashed, the illusions she wrapped around me all taken down. She came to Beacon Hill to fall in love with a poet, she came because of a poet, she came because of me, and I failed, I suppose. I did not be a poet for her. She wanted someone to fall in love

with spirit, with her soul, to make her feel worthy, and I, with my cheap Bohemianism of the rent-raising party smashed the dream in her face. I should be very stoic, and say that they come and go, the little girls come up here with their eyes closed, with their hearts on their proverbial and fullchested sweaters, and they stay to see another dream break. I should not be in agony, it is her, falling asleep night after night, in her unworthy bed, filled with doubts of God and the reason for the world, filled with longing because people only look at their faces. So they stop wearing lipstick and pretty clothes, they stop combing their hair, they take up poets who they feel will see them, and the poets such as I see no one, and yet need everyone. We want to be detached, we want to live in prison, where we can see the world and not be in it, and the girls come in with keys, they let themselves in, and they find nothing but a shaggy little me who sleep on dirty sheets, who have lovers, who drink too much dime beer, and wear dirty pants to the rest of the world. They want priests to fall in love with, it should not be me. And yet, I Miss her, I miss the little face with no paint on it, and the hard long hand in me, and the quivering, always quivering mouth. She asked me, if I knew what it was to get up every morning afraid, what is she afraid of, I will keep her in dirty rooms, but she is young and stupid and needs me, I suppose that I why I feel for her, because she needs someone, and I feel it is me. At least she needs someone who can see her. I have urged her to become an actress, to put herself into something great, to dedicate her shabbiness. I do remember the magic minutes of makebelieving we had together, the time we were huddled up on a couch in a Harvard Dormitory, listening to modern music by Jerome Morross. We didn't even speak, and the nights I would see her off at the Charles St. Subway, still kissing her on the left cheek, and the night we lay on my living room floor, on the blue, silver striped pillow, I have thrown out, and when she read me a part from Giradoux, and when she wore my old clothes and looked lovely in a barron, and how she went skating on the Public Gardens, in my overcoat and her beret, and how I chased after her, thinking she was Great Garbo, and that I would inspire her to great mystery and enchantment. But it is all dead, she saw me too close. People should not unless they are desperate and fully aware of the chances, get too close to other people. See people through a grey veil, grey for faults, and you will love them in your heart forever, think of them always with warmth, but see people in the daytime, with the sun on their faces, and you will run away at the blackheads and whiskers and acne, and grease. I could look at Rita in the daytime as that is when she wanted me to, but she had to see me by candlelight in rooms papered with the poets. Thus she is gone, and still I am not gone from her. It is two months to the night that I began this soul sieve, and I am not proud, maybe slightly because of its length.

Monday, March 21, 1955

I take this time out, because I am or have been trying to write and do not want to now, I want to run out into the dream of a movie, or go downtown and buy beer. Today is the first day that I have actually tried to do creative writing, apart from this journal, and I find it torturous. If I Only could be free, and yet I would not, for the happiness of the whole world, I would not. It has been the enervation, if that is the right word, of this past weekend that I think has weakened me. Also I did not get out of bed until after noon, but tomorrow I shall cure that. I shall put the typewriter beside the bed again, and that shall strengthen me. This weekend was spent in Providence, amid martinis and Chartreuse liquor, and Seabreezes and Zinfandel, and homebrew beer, and parties. I have not answered the door to the knockers this morning, which is a step and again. But I get no joy from the writing, it is labor, and there is no enthusiasm I go to it as a duty, as a job, and I find no solace only emotion that I can't even describe. I shall take a walk to Scharaff's and buy some cookies, and a newspaper. It might be that because I have shut myself off from the world that I am shriveling up inside.

Tuesday Morning, March 22

I have begun with this morning my new schedule. Since it is only three weeks before I must return to work somewhere, it is intense, and I shall get something done if I persevere. I get up at 9 and begin writing in this journal by 9:30 daily, revising and adding new entries until I have written one hundred pages, and then until the end of the summer I shall work on it, perfecting and polishing. I don't know why, but it might make money. I work on the journal every morning until 12:30. Until 2, I write letters, eat lunch, entertain, and possibly walk. I return to the apartment and read or study the Iliad until six, with supper and trip to the library until 7 or 7:30. I then spend the remainder of the night in writing or in technical exercise. It is a good schedule but I doubt if I will keep it as accurately as I have written down here,

Thursday night, 8:10, March 24

As might be expected I have not kept my schedule. Today I got up from the sheets at 1:15. Why I do not know. I was awake at nine, went back and dreamed of cockroaches, with green spotted wings, I killed as many as I could. Bob Greene or Vincent was here at 1:30 and we went to Harvard Square on this pleasant sunfilled day. I bought an edition of Edna Millay's "Second April" for 50¢. I flipped a coin again and it came down heads, and so it joins my shelf. I have more of her work than anyone, Pound second. I do not care or regard Millay's poetry as anything near great, and Pound is my idol, at the very least Personae surpasses, without any just comparison, what Millay has done. I also went to a poetry reading of one Mr. Edwin Honig, reciting from his new book, "The Moral Circus". Most of his work is not good, smelling of Dylan Thomas at its best, and he reads in what to me is a dull conversational tone, no fire, which is what is necessary to keep people in a green hot room awake. Poetry is bringing itself back to the ears of the "people", is being made more precise. The bunk of it can be sifted out by having it read aloud.

I am writing to Black Mountain College for a work and talent scholarship. This, if I am accepted, will be the decisive point in my life. I shall work hard at field and farm labors, but I shall be working towards the learning of this craft, which is all that really matters. I am sending the letter off tonight air mail, asking them for catalogue, and telling them of the unusual circumstances in my history, i.e. already having received my A.B. I hope that by making these facts clear at the beginning, that I shall win favor, and thus entry. To think of it, on a mountain in North Carolina for years.

Went to Earle Pilgrim's nervous over being returned the money he owes. Met his wife outside and I asked her, she gave me $3.00, and the rest each week. The important thing though is that I met there Dolores Valle, another B.C. School of Education girl. She is a Rita Nolan type, but much more genuine, much more naïve, and truthful. We walked in the rain, had tea together at Hayes Bickford, she loves cafeterias, and enjoyed her wistfulness and her girlity. She too, like Marie and Rita, has severe doubts about Our Holy Mother The Church. If B.C. only knew what they are letting through its blessed fields. And yet, if anyone makes the place known, as the breeding ground of artists and sundry, it shall be us, the infidels, the disbelievers, the scorners of Her and her conventions. I am afraid that we are as we are partly because of our rebellion against the usual Boston College student graduate, a bodyworthless.

Dolores told me of a lecture she went to given by Fr. Donovan, one of the deans, in which he said. "We have the Truth, we maybe do not have the physical equipment, and the scholars and the genius that other universities possess. But we have the Truth." The only truth that Boston College has ever produced is the hatred in us of that type of statement. I am going into the night to mail what I hope is the salvation of my life. Oh Black Black is the mountain I shall live on.

Saturday, 12:30 A.M. March ?

I sit down here, as dramatically as it sounds, with a heavy heart. It is so heavy that it will not let me write out what I feel. I want his step on the stairs, I want his voice in my ears, I want his face before my eyes. And I will not let these things come to be. I do not want human love, and yet I am so lonely and hurting without it. What is he doing now, yes, dear reader, you ask who HE is, and I shall tell you, it is the someone that I have always written about. He has not left me, it is god I love, and yet, if love means this, if love means cruelty and agony and loneliness, I can not take it. I shall try and go alone, I shall pretend that love is dead, that he is dead, that I will never have his body again (and downstairs now I hear a key turning in someone's door, and for one knifing minute, I think it is his feet on the stairs) I know he is not dead. Somewhere in Boston tonight, someone else is putting their mouth on his, he is looking at someone else, I will be restrained and classical, I will be the inscription over Delphi, "Nothing in Excess" in translation.

I have discovered now that this is my mode of expression, it is on these pages that my heart is speaking forth. I see this as simply another of my incessant dreams, I see this not as reality for today is chaos, and yet to hear his feet on the stairs would be equal and worth the confusion.

I shall go on pretending he is dead. And to soothe me, I shall read the achievement of a man, a man who triumphed over his country, and his religion, but I remember, he had Nora, he had a love, man can not live without Nora.

Sunday morning, March 27, 1955

It is still no better. Rub my heart, it hurts. I would that

someone would rub my heart, it hurts. Can I do it? Do I have the strength to go throughout this chaos of world without a lover? Will I wander with Mahler? And if he comes back, I will not take him, I will not open up my arms to him. I have had love longer than anyone in my world has had it, and I do not want it in a diluted potion now. I will not take the splinters of love, I will not take it simply because I do not have the strength to walk in chaos alone. I have had the full mouth of love, and I will not take a handshake now. I have stayed in bed the last two days for something near thirty hours, and I know that this hurt has to pass, I wonder how long it will be; and whether I will come out in triumph.

JOURNAL FOR MONDAY, AUGUST 17

I do not think so. I do not think that love survives man; he destroys what he has labored to build, what he has stayed awake nights over to be in the dawn, he breaks. Tear down, tear down, for all sides where he labors, he is met by fat resistance and inertia. And the challenge is to lie in its arms, and kiss it to life. To take inertia and put the electric charge in, thru sex? To meet the rock and by his body heat make lava. Let it come down what the fingers stroked. We pull down for some perverse reason. And this is not a personal destructive urge, no defense is necessary, age will calm us, make us patient, but who wants it. Why do we want the vortex of the tornado? But no questions should be asked, let us take it as we take lying in the sun. And if love does not survive, we will build another. I want a love affair, therefore I make one. I work on love as I would a canvas, or a poem, oh but that is wrong, for love takes us, I cannot stop believing it, that it takes us as the vortex does, and now when we are stopped at storm center, fatigue takes us. I will not allow old love to take me. Simply because it is old, and my blood is dried on its teeth, I will not put my head in again. I will stand outside and shake my belly so it is wrapped in the veil of myself. One finally finds after all that there is no one but the self, that this is what must be brought strong, so that its comforts are secondary, and the comfort of love shall be nothing more than a warmth in bed, and not a life to plunge the self in. There shall be no indwelling, and if this way leads to disaster, the disaster of the lonely room, there shall be no guilt, no scream of I was wrong! I should have knelt the self down, never that, no matter how dark the room, or how big the empty bed you toss on, never again the fist against the head to destroy the self. Let the other, let love die if need be, but the interior, that inner possession shall be kept at full force, and let those who want to warm their hands at it, in, let them be everywhere, but tend that fire, of the spirit.

Journal
Today is September 8th, 1956. It is a Saturday and and for no reason I begin again an interrupted journal. I want this to be the chronicle of an interior life, of an interior and its reaction, its approach to and aversion from the little universes that travel in the same orbit of this microcosm, ourself, myself.

I have returned to a small town outside of Boston, Massachusetts. Its name is Milton. It is my home town, and up to the age of 20, I returned here nearly every night to sleep. In two weeks, I shall have left Milton again either to live in Boston or to return to North Carolina, to a place called Black Mountain College. I am not going to waste words describing that to you, read an old catalogue in your local library, and you will find out a little, at least of its physical set-up. It is a cool day and my sister called it Fallish.

I am not much at peace in the small sense today, but my interior is at a peace of sorts. As Olson told me, my ethos is firm, is finely structured, and he led me, so that I believe him, and know, most times, that I walk on strong ground, and the smell there gives me comfort, and patience. The patience to endure the small collisions that always bang up one's universe. No matter, there is green grass on this stretch, an old desert cannot even be seen today. And there is no mist, no rose-colored glasses. Patience. Patience to wait until six o'clock tonight when my mother has ended her near-compulsory supper, and I can go in town and look up Spicer and the Dunns and see Steve Jonas' redecorated apartment, and I shall also read my new poems, my summer poems from Black Mountain College. And I shall forego love on Charles Street, shall pass it up in the dark because I am patient, patient until next week when my lover and I go to Provincetown and try to rebuild a relationship that we have nearly destroyed. That is why I have come home from Black Mountain, that is why I wait in this little sunny room in Milton, wait for re-building, wait for love to, and then I shall, quick, quick, spin the gold wire around it, and trap all three of us inside, so when I am fat and bald and with false teeth, love will still sleep on my pillow, as it does not now, when I am thin and shiny and with soft brown hair. Of course, as Duncan says, Love is a pretend game, so we might as well play it that way, and do a good job, and the warmth, the sweat of another intimate human being helps us endure, as long as we do not forego our own green path. But I do not always see the joy in front of me, and some perverseness in my nature refuses it when it kisses me. Of course, I am in love with a shit, and we are two men and both want to dominate and take the aggressor's part, and seduce each other, so now this tension has brought us to such a weary battlefield, that we have rested all summer, and begin again. Our bodies have not been given to each other for over four months, and in a way, I am glad, because I have saved mine, knowing that to give it to any one but him, or a strange potential woman, would be a waste, so I save, although he does not, he squanders his lovely back on strangers, but his back shall be brought down in ecstasy on me, and soon. He shall be unknown to himself and his arms shall lift me, and his mouth shall enter mine, and the fire that has been growing these four months shall be charged over and ignite him, and his knowing shall be lost, he shall be brought low in desire. So I have patience because this rich life of waiting nourishes me and grows a green path. And this is why I do not return to Black Mountain, because the spider in me has no web to spin, and there is no angry hornet to catch. And this is the most exciting part of love, the plan one makes to be loved, the traps one sets for love, and I too must be an angry hornet enough and have mystery on my wings so that his perverse mind will want to spin to pin down my buzzing, and that when I give my fire, he will glory in its winning, like the male he is, like the male I am.

Written by John Wieners in Boston
1955–56 — entailing his trials
as a poet and a lover.

Beautiful Saint
of the underworld ~~underworld~~, of the underg
Lamantia, ~~it is you~~ ~~unheralded~~
it is you
~~night~~ I ~~am~~ Try~~ing~~ to ~~reach~~ in the cavern
~~his soul,~~ I am Trying to reach, heral
~~sat,~~
~~s you~~

~~I am Trying to~~
~~ar~~ screeching in the wind.

s your soul, I am Trying to ~~balm~~ reach
you needed it, as if the cross
which I sit, is not enough and you
in me by Dean, from some Byzantin
iest, swinging at his hip or around
his neck.

tight rubess, the gems of amythst, or jade
~~se~~ are yours. The white dove flying
at eventide
ese are yours. The Mediterannean,
a pure white sea. The blue shit.
These are yo

*moths my only company;

August 8, 1965

Sitting in the tough LA moonlight, with the light from Wally's studio falling on these pages; the sound of motors below dying on Beverly Glen Blvd. The air above alive with crickets, and falling leaves.

The breath of some invisible spectre whistles through the trees. A plane roars over the mountains, heading into LA Terminal. Like Rome for the trains.

Somewhere in this night, beautiful women bare their olive shoulders to the moon, unknowing. And handsome men lie in bed, waiting.

I wait too, for life to open its windows and let me in. I wait too, in the unknowing night, for the sea to wash over some far beach, on foreign shores, and I am there to see it.

I wait too for the companion to come out of the moonlight and we walk together in the soft air to some future destination, simple in its design. In that it be constructed of one and easy to penetrate. Easy to overcome and easy to leave.

The cat comes, meowing out of the vines, afraid of my pen, moving in the darkness. Sniffing these pages.

Wally comes along the path, his flashlight a beacon in the wood. We talk awhile, our tempers flare at Olson's name. It is no good, his resentment of certain things. I would like to sweep them aside and show him the greater expanse of love between men, without reference to creed, aesthetics or condition. It is right to stamp aside the enemy, but friends must be endured, no matter what cost, as they are few, and others so many and powerful.

They do not know this, and appearances must be maintained. Of unity and strength.

The cat comes back. She is going wild and a white one stalks her out on the driveway. I suppose this is what love is, or friendship in Art.

She resumes her position on the rocks.

And the white one comes up on the boards, and gazes at her, the two of them hypnotized in the moonlight.

It is that kind of night. And Wally's cutting board sounds in the studio, and I go back, to join him in the compassion that is love.

Or rather he comes out, and off we go to our simple destination in the trees.

I do not know what monster next may appear out of the leaves. Or stalk its prey in the night. I hope it is not me.

North Star
shining alone in the night,
                over Beverly Hills,
in my stolen bathrobe and shirt,
                in my borrowed house,
I think of you cold and aloof,
                withdraw from men,
while I am enwrapped
                in their doings.

I think of you and Laurence,
                Through the haze of drugs,
drink and beautiful bodies.

                How you both were removed,
while I am entrapped

in their being.

Every gesture of body, every movement
of hand moves my heart, too.

to desire and darker hurt

Only the light from Wally's studio

below sustains me

in this hour of wilderness.

HAIKU

It's not what at the time affects you.
It's afterwards that hurts me.

Tijuana Border

Sitting up at the Mexico border in the early morning sunlight,
just north of Tijuana, preparing to cross the border for the
second time.

Mary enters the car and begins brushing her hair in a
symphony of gold light. Her voice is like music, light as a
rippling river. Her boyfriend is out back, fixing clothes in
the trunk. He will soon join us.

Along with a third, Danny Russell, whom I first met
yesterday in LA at Wally Berman's. Well on the trip and
new adventure.

Stumble bum stumbles in:
We start but have not yet begun.

2.　　　Nestor

One of those dreary little border towns one always reads about in books but which are worse, the only consolation one has is that other writers have endured it.

In the Mountains of Mexico

South of the Border
  down Mexico way,

      I cant break away from his
           charms,
      I cant break away from his
           arms,
   South of the Border, down Mexico
   I cant break away –
   from his ch-arms,
   I cant break away
   from his harms, I cant break away
               from his arms
    Alarms! Charms! I cant break away

from this mountain echo of Mexico.

2.

A sudden rainstorm
electric breaks over the radio,
drowning out the current.

        A sudden rainstorm
drowns out the radio, sends static

over the airwaves.
A sudden rainstorm
moves in the mountain,
causing window-wipers
to wipe away his face.

I cant break away

from his charms, in the mountains of Mexico

3.
Pass thru it now and move over into dark, green hills

White stones with white markings on it.

White lightening in the sky.

White hope, whole in the hole of Mexico

down South of the Border,

Mexicali way.

August 12, 1965

4.
Life can be a dream, you know
with white lightening in the sky.

Order of Books in the Library

Pound
Olson
Williams
Lawrence

       To Mike
         in Tucson
I'm here with a guy from the Bronx, baby,
a girl from Brooklyn,
and a guy from Queens:
and
You know what that means.
          Jack

Honeysuckle

Drummond King walks in the afternoon light
I sit in the warmth of this chair, waiting
for him to return. The mountains are before us
I admire his warm, brown flank and shoulder
I cannot see him under the trees. He is lost
to me. I will go swimming and maybe he will
join me. He has gone into the woods.

I see him across the road, pass through
the fields. The shedding of the leaves
obscure part of his body from me.

He is now within my full view. He has gone

into the pool. I hear him splash.

No he is out, I see his head over the top
of the flowers. A lazy hawk circles

in the sky.

  "Drum," the water goes.
  "Drum," my heart pounds.
  "Drum," the mountains say as they
look down on us.
    "Finger mountain," he said, pointing
to one sliver where he camped out, last
winter and saw the snow. In Tucson,
Arizona.

Arizona

The light falls horizontally on the mountains
The congruity of all things falls as light
on these mountains of time, causing things
to float together, past, present and future
is one.

  1) The bird swings on its perch,

  2) The boy picks up his bathing suit
in the swimming pool

  3) The girl runs across the lawn.

  4) The poet sits dreaming in the dawn

waiting for the right word to call,
the light to fall.

2)
   The poet must summon words as his defense,
against the world; and for it.
   This is a magic journal and I have
hoarded words for a long time to hide in
it; to put in use, now that late summer
is here, and chestnuts fall, the sea wind
rises in the desert, the light falls across these mountains.

The Sun Valley Jump.

And discovers caves that ~~are~~ hard ~~to getting~~ into;
worse to get out of; oh love!

   Sonja Henri skis down slopes
      of green valleys

   in hope that time will dissolve

The memories of Jack Oakie.

      She has and is in

pursuit of; love, sweet love.

     John Payne, too
dissolves in that eager fame

     for time.

To Lionel Phillips

Time, they say, must best of us capture,
    And travel and battle and gems and gold
No more can kindle the ancient rapture,
    For even the youngest of hearts grows old,
But in you, I think, the boy is not over;
    So take this medley of ways and wars
As the gift of a friend and a fellow-lover
    Of the fairest country under the stars.
              J.B.

Milton

In the middle of the night, always
it returns to me, this beauty
of poetry, the moon flashing
across the wine-dark sea, like your eye,
The lights in it, at dinnertime.
When I smile at a particularly
pleasant memory, able to live it again.
And the joy of that transmits to you,
sitting across the table from me, my mother.

Beautiful Saint   of the underground

Philip Lamantia,
     it is you
         in the caverns
of the night, I am trying to herald.
It is you tonight, lost in Paris

I am trying to
~~I hear screeching in the wind~~

It is your soul, I am trying to reach
as if you needed it, as if the cross
on which I sit, is not enough and yours.
Given me by Dean, from some Byzantine
priest, swinging at his hip or around
                          his neck.

The tight rubies, the gems of amethyst, or jade.
These are yours. The white dove flying
                    at eventide.
These are yours. The Mediterranean,
The pure white sea. The blue shit.

Holy

Silence, holy unmoving mouths
of my beloveds, holy faces shining
in the night, holy light.

Holy plane flying in the stars
Holy moon rising, holy sun setting
Hole of the planets between which

Nothing lives. Holy death. This last
The hardest to bear. Holy friends gone there.
Holy songs haloing their heads lost to sight.

Hotel Blues
For Jack Spicer

Pass by this room, stranger.
Heartbreak hides within it.
Tears and wine, brandy.
Will not stop the wound, nor staunch the blood.
Lean not on this bell. It brings only hell.
Pass by this room, stranger.
The young lead in battalions.
Tarry not in this hallway, boy.
Hurry on by.

Hold not your hands to the light, here
friend, skip the moon.
Get off at the ground floor
        and keep on moving
          right out the door.
to the fresh air.
Friend, pass on by.
Fit no key in this lock. Nor look over my transom.
You'll see only death sitting on the bed.
Stretching out her long hair into the moon.

Hotel Blues
For Jack Spicer
Pass by this room, stranger.
Heartbreak hides within it.
Pass by this door.
Tarry not in this hall, boy.
Hurry on down

Hold not your hands to the light, here
friend, skip the moon.
Get off the ground floor
          and keep on going.
friend, pass right out the door.

Fit no key in this lock friend. Nor look over my transom.
You'll see only death sitting on the bed.
Stretching out her long hair unto the moon.

I have worn myself out on this world,
Worn my face down. on sidewalks.
I have shed my soul to the moon.

Like A Rolling Stone

I came home to this house, feeling beautiful –
one week ago tonight, and now I do not
feel beautiful – these people have
crushed me – have crushed out the
beautiful.
      They have divided me with
their small talk, with their asylums,
prisons and poisons. They
have crushed out the beauty.
      My uncles, aunts – the women
especially, my mother and sister.
They have snickered in bitterness, with
envy at the misfortunes of others.
They have stared with blind eyes
at television. They have risen in the
morning to no new day. They have not
changed their pattern for me.

The men practice drunkenness and
the women frustration.

They taste my success but do not
share the growing, Only the harvesting
is theirs and they seek out only the
sensational blossoms for their own.

They leave the bitter wine which is
best untasted. And they have
crushed out the beautiful in my soul.
I am an empty shard now while I stay
here. I am a broken blossom on the
stem, dying in the wilderness desert
of their lives. I cannot plant new trees. They
do not listen. Will not see the new leaves.
Find only weeds and broken blossoms.
They have taken my friends by the neck
and snap them off from the stem
which is me. And I am a pure
stalk, growing in the wilderness.

I am still an abundant vine
but cannot grow in this house. Cannot
come to fruit here in this wilder-
ness. Without friends. With only
friends, far away to nourish me.

2.

Let me get away quick. Let me
grow apart from this house. The
priests have talked to them. They do not
listen. The poets have preached. The
celebrities stare from their
glossy pages. They do not know
what it means. What price we have
paid who get away.

They think it is all a game. That

we are the lucky ones. They do now know
we went away for a reason. That their
lives are not enough. That their men
have not supplied them with substance
for their lives. They are afraid. To
die, be injured, suffer, put in jail,
through the mill. They have worked in the
mills but not walked the streets. They
have sat in their living rooms and not
danced the night, watching the entert-
ainment of shysters and hustlers from
far away, they have let others get their
kicks for them.
    And they have watched in envy,
and bitterness and frustration.
They do not try. And turn on all
others who come near them, and are
different and have tried. They listen
to the planes at night and wonder
what makes these people fly. They
are peasants. And I am one of them.
But will not stay here. To die beneath
their feet. I would rather be corn
and threshed out in the marketplace.
I would rather be weighed and found
wanting than stay here within their
wilderness. At least I have been on
the scales.
    I have felt the weights beneath my
feet, the weight above my head, the noose
around my neck. But I have not
flinched. And I have not regretted
    I slid over the abyss and woke up
screaming. I went hungry, and
penniless and homeless. And I regret

nothing. Je regrette rien. Edith Piaf
sang. Le petite sparrow of the streets,
and my father loved her.

And they supplied me with a home,
and food and clothes, only so people
would not point at them and say,
"Unworthy parents". And they have
been unworthy. And I have not
pointed at them, until now when
they have crushed the beautiful
in my soul, which I brought
home from far places. At great
pain and with much trouble.

They ignore me and go
about their own business which is not
business at all, but only habit.

We create the world anew. We
go out on our own. We est-
ablish old traditions of heroes
and travels in the face of these workers
who do not know what the world is about,
who do not know what a gift it is to live,
what a challenge, and
how short-lived. How eternity is found
in a second.

How the face of God shines in their own.
And they are not cheap, and must not treat
themselves or others as such.

3.

I would play Edith Piaf now on the phonograph,
but am afraid to. Fear is a constituent
of their lives and they breed it in others,
in all they touch, their children, and
dogs, flowers and lawns. All, bred

in fear. Rose-patterns on the wall, out
of fear of the cosmos, its chaos.
    For Xaos came first, called out
of order – the order of our
lives in the face of their
chaos
    Of destruction, building itself up
in the thousand, minute daily acts
of their lives, they do without thinking.
        I must get away from them. They

have infected me.

    Bring me back to the wilderness
of lives, without order in their eyes,

        Reading Duncan's <u>Adam's Way</u>
                    To Charles Olson
A spirit rises from this book
that is dear to me. The past remains
as a rock to harbor our dreams,
as <u>floats</u> upon the streets of time.

You are near me in this night. Near as moon
that shines forever in your eyes
                that will die

But shine now as beacons in the dawn.

Oh break on, forever, gentle man
            in your dreams and mine

Don't read
Debtors plaguin my door,
Old friends gone sore sour
Aint in to the world no more.

~~My mind got lost in the thirties,~~
~~it went to war in the forties,~~
~~by the fifties I found it again~~
~~only to lose it by sixty-seven~~

~~For good, for good~~
~~Goodbye old friends and debtors,~~
~~old girls along the road.~~
~~May the seventies be better.~~

Dont read

Oh what agony to be without someone to love.

To share the room with photographs of

The Abundance of Autumn,

and be alone,

with only the Fountains of Rome as a memory.

the Pincio, Villa Medici and Belvedere Gardens
    still burn brightly in my mind,
  but nightly I wander there alone
    with only a burning pain in my stomach.

It's just a room with a bed in it,
but it's all I have,
and bells ring outside the window
and friends take time to stop by,

sometimes, if I'm lucky.
It's not much, but all I have.
   No cigarettes, and chill in the air.
   not even a room with a view.

But my mind's clear, and I dont take drugs,
continually, which is a help.
And I'm not in jail, and can pay the rent,
even if two weeks behind.

So add things up, and I'm still a saint,
even if the dream's busted,
or tarnished at the edges.
The dream holds up, even busted.

There was cold at the beginning, and there's
less here now. There was drink at the
beginning and there's less here now.
There was love at the beginning and
there's less here now.

No cigarette tastes as sweet as wanting one.
I dont stick needles in my arm anymore.
The flesh doesn't hang off my arm.
                    (like it used to

oh blue veins that stick out, where before they were
                    collapsed.

(Oh lapsed, moral vein

ANEW

From the desolate landscape of the past,
into the slums of future time,
I come bearing garlands of our summer.

From the drama of drugged yesterdays,
into the barren plains of tomorrow,
I come bearing hope of today.

From the death of all living regret
into the canyons of what destiny
I come bearing now the dreams anew.

ANEW

From the desolate landscape of past dreams
into slums of future time
I come bearing garlands of summer

From the death of drugged yesterday,
Into the barren plains of tomorrow
I come bearing hopes from May

From the earth of living regret,
into the canyons of what destiny
I come bearing now dreams anew.

II ALONE

Sustained by poetry, fed anew
by its fires to return from madness,
the void does not beckon as it used to.
Littered with syllables, the road does not loom
as a chasm – the hand of strangers on other
doors does not hurt. The breath of gods
does not desert, but clouds large
as a dream's, a prairie within our dream,
to which return, when we need to.
Oh blessed plain, oh pointed chasm.

Sustained by poetry, fed anew
by its fires to return from madness,
the void does not beckon as it used to.
Littered by syllables, the road does not lurch
to a chasm, but lingers here. The hand of strangers
does not hurt, on other doors; the breath of gods

do not desert us, but looms large on the horizon
as a cloud bank over fires; the silly laughter

of girls does not irritate, but is listened to
as the measure of muses; as a road within our dream,
where prairies lead us, to a dream when we need to.
Oh blessed cavern; oh pointed abyss.

There are some girls who dance the night away, like Gloria
and some who die right away, like my mother.

Chapter on <u>Women</u>

All witches were lovely women once.
Dian
Jan and hotel room, on stage at burlesque, traveling
across country,
Sheila Plant de Nine Jones
Jan Jones

Chapter on Place
San Francisco

At the Posners

On the rose rug "men dance on deathless fact."
Centuries past still, women go
collecting China.

And cooking meals. All love is there
gathered on the piano
in a sunspot.

The roar of motors drowned and Buffalo
seems miles away. It is England
and the timeless bone
of China is gathered
in a poet's words.

In the communion of spirits that feeds the brain
nourish the spirit we find
a circle of angels or saints
that sing new tunes, without words or voices.
only their mouths are open
we cannot hear them.

The nuances of light upon their curls distract
our eyes. The simplicity of mind that dictates
this confession. I think we're mad
most of the time, ringing phones, reading
papers, trying to hold our own, in a world
that kills.

Love-Song

Too late you vanished out of my dreams,
You may be sorry now,
It's over, all over but
        how about me?

You found somebody new –
        what am I to do,
But still remember you,
        when you've forgotten me.
And later, much later, baby
will climb up on your knee,
and put her arms around your neck,
        how about me?

A gentleman caller – after midnight
in his white Porsche
with heroin upon his knee.

A radio next door, and wind
at the window, whispering
will he come?

May-be, maybe.
Wait and see,
    little baby.

Sept 27, 1965 –
I don't have the capacity for
poetry, only a longing for life that drives
me mad, in these confined circumstances.
    The hand of heroin writes these words, and

yet I don't consider myself a dope-fiend, as
I do not spend my time looking for it,
as before; nor do I have the money.

Now that life no longer provides the means
for poetry. I am caught within my mind.
And it is not enough. With the shock-treat-
ments and drugs. It never was, even
before.
     But now it is worse. I lack the concentration
yet I will learn. I lack the discipline.
Still I will learn it. Give me the means
to find these things and make them
a daily part of my life. I need them, if I am
to continue to grow.
     Right now, I wait for my friend's white
Porsche to drive up, and will he, is all
that concerns my mind.

"those who are faithful know only the trivial side of
love: it is the faithless who know love's trag-
edies." Oscar Wilde.   PoDGray

The New World

When after midnight, when poetry is always
nearer, I look out my window, and see the
moon of the parking lot light shine down
on the pavement, that is greased with the oil
of a hundred cars parked there by day, or
night; and I hear in the distance
over Lake Erie the hoot of a steamer or

train – then I know the spirit or silence
which permits poetry to be, has fallen over
the world and the mind; and a flood of
sister memories rise within my mind; or
upon my mind's eye; or movie screen of
the soul – and the past is returned to me.
The glorious moments of the past, which are
few and far between; the dross falls away,
the agony of living is worth it. All the trying
moments of life are paid for by the few,
precious images that return. The New
Year's Eve with friends, the darkened room
where fiddles played, bells rang,
tooted whistles over the river. Nothing
disturbs me, the coolness of a palace
stair, turned into a museum, the sunlight
melted through an upper window of
yellow gloss softens the balustrade,
and one's steps return to a
Sunday afternoon upon its stone.

    The gathering of friends within a room,
the softness of the moon, the greenness of a
tree, the flight of birds on the air, whirling
away through time, specks of song,
melody rushing to the ear, again –
the dawn alive with chatter; the crowing
of cocks, tolling of bells, rushing of tires
that is ever present in our towns and
cities now.

    The sad faces of friends; these haunt
the night. The words of artists; how our writers
neglect this now.
    The sun seen over the sea; the very sea
itself, its waves forever beating on every

shore – how all of this is reflected,
                    recollected
in the moonlight of a lamp light
shining down on the parking lot, after
midnight.
          And how quickly gone, all time is,
when one's mind leaves that little light
and returns to the room, where ironically
life is. Or is it, life at all? Or just
a simulation of life, under which reality
hides. The real hides itself under cover
of things; upon the mind's screen lies
the true nature of things; there the
flux of time presents the objects
which endure; and persists in that
they return so quickly, when one is free
of the world and its demand. All poets must
exist within that space; there is no longer
any excuse. They must do so or die.
Even the necessity of economics must
not prevent this. Even if they must
die doing so. They must die, in pursuit
of this. For that is the nature of a
poet; and pursuit of the poet. If he
does not do this, then he is no longer a
poet – and by doing other things is
an other thing.

    Even the pursuit of love is a hindrance
to the poet; the desire for food or shelter
all hindrances – only the pursuit
of food for the spirit, shelter for the mind, thought from the
      spirit – all these must be experienced; pursuit for space
and the tenacity of thought is so tenuous
so fine that if lost if distracted

for a moment the thread is broken;
the memory shattered; the image lost.
Ah, the weary burden of a poet. No wonder
Their nerves are strained like steel, but so thin
They vibrate in the wind to every nuance and cannot
be seen by any but the most experienced
eye. Ah, love that must be passed by in
pursuit of the poem.

Ah experience that must be
paused by, for experience of the poem.
Ah, paused by, listen to me again, sound to me, that I
may sing your song.

2.

the only thing about this note is by the time the first
image was written of New Year's Eve, or
the museum balustrade, the flood of
sister memories had disappeared
down the steps of "time", back into the
mind, from which they arose – and
thus, this essay is living
proof of the evanescence of the mind,
or imagination. How fragile and
evanescent it is, how little retains,
remains, and how much is gone,
disappeared forever. Or is it? That
is the metrics with which I am con-
cerned. To return forever the lost mind
to its plane, which is fleeting and temporal, too

But which does endure in imagination.
The community of thought, host of angels,
they used to call it. Muses, or mother

of memory, itself.   Not allegory, but
symbol, as Yeats and Blake used it.
Thus disregard the memory, and rely on
some other mechanism of the mind,
which presents image and does endure,
out of time, which after all, is only
an illusion of the mind. Or does
time exist, outside the mind? And
can create and destroy the mind, too.
        Ah, sad, suffering destroying mind

that can create time, too; that is all I know.
the mind is all I want to know.
            And need to know on the earth of man.
        That is all ye need to know; truth and beauty
                        exists outside our minds.
"Truth is beheld by the intellect; beauty
by the imagination," Joyce said

3.
        Not compte enough. The Known is never complete
enough. It is the unKnown which completes me.
For which I hunger. For which I lack
words. Or mind. Oh, complete me. Dictate to me
words of my soul. I have listened for you
long enough. And yet not long enough. The
moon is never complete. But partial
to our eye. I hunger for the lost side of the moon,
the new moon is the new meter.

As I lie in the dark, I dream of the future.
The contemplation of the past. My candles
have burned out; I cannot see.
        Hunger breeds inspiration. When I am

fed, I do not create;
    Lovers lie whispering next door.
    Upstairs the poet walks on creaking
floors, after mid-night, his inspiration, their hands meet on
    the telephone
burnt out, his soul burned by flames he
cannot quench.
    Whence comes this thought, these
words. My words are dictated me, as if
on some unknown machine, they tele-
type across my brain. Not all of them.
The word is the only world; the world is only

a word; but it is more than it. It is a never
quenching flame, that can burn you out
and take all you have, and still ask for
more, plead for more quickly. It can
take every emotion you lavish on an object and exhaust it
so quickly that you fall dying on the
roadside; bed so quickly, you murmur,
only to rise again the next morning to
feed it again. To feed on you; feed on it.
That is the only answer. Be impartial,
cold to everything and it dies quickly.
But be cold and you die quickly.

                John Wieners
for what it's worth. A bad   Sept 29, 1965
  entry full of sloppy thinking out of tiredness.

To Harvey

I like Sunday nights after you've been
                    here.
I can use your perfume and pretend you
                    are near
My eyes are bright in the night.
Why can't I have a man of my own?

Your wife's necklace is around my neck and
Even though I do shave I can pretend
                    I'm a woman for you
And you make love to me like a man.
I hear you say, why man he doesn't even have
any teeth, when I take out my plate.
But I will make it up to you in other ways.
I will write this poem.

I will wash my hair for you.
Do my fingernails   be as thoroughly
            elegant as I can.

Memories and Heartache

Borne aloft, and carrying no other name,
            than its own.
        into the moon. Mist

from the pipe of dreams.

gone Heaven-ward.

    <u>Kicking</u>
   The World <u>is</u> the Mind
is a blurred photograph, or
newsreel, taking pictures not here.
    obscured
     on earth.

Mind blurred moon shot. Or Prado.

Ocean dissolved. Planet Shrouded.
    White spectre

risen from the sea.
    How to tie it up
      as a vision

    or demon demands The art of poetry.

    Not heroin,

But spirit or ghost free from the bog
    of mystery.
     Heaven's pit

Dear Charlie,

    how glad I am you got away. But how I miss you,
in little ways.

Hunting Cigarette Butts

is a vain occuptain, after the rain. It sharpens the brain, though
to look in doorways, what hides down cracks in the cement,
under cars, theatre lobbys.

    But it never pays off. (Too much of an effort) And they are
       always wet, soggy,
sticky. Cigar-ooneys, how I have looked for you. How my
       tongue ached,
how I longed to hear a car drive up and find a friend in it,
who had one. Or a loan. Or approach strangers. Risky to do
       that.
You might get detained.   After the rain, in a doorway.
    Or you might hear a door open, and he would be there,
with a pack in his hands. A blessed cigarette.
    To light the dark, to carry with you to sleep,
to hunt thru the night. A strike.
    There's one with its motor running, they used
to say in New York. And the party goes on, upstairs;
glasses clinked, stuffed in pockets, grass squashed
a glass. Who would know someone waits

downstairs for your cigarette butts. After the rain,
when the streets are bare. Doorways, too. That's a
good place to look. But not enough. There is always
a woman standing there, waiting for a bus, or
a train, a man.

Who are these bastards who think because
they publish a book for you, they have done
enough?

Or it's a lit corner, and you can't stoop
down to pick it up with all these people
around, or you're crossing the street and
you can't stop to get it, with all these car
headlights shining on you. It's bad enough
they even have to see you, in thread-bare coat,
etc (but at least you got one) with long

hair, etc, but at least you had a job once. Etc.
and you got a warm room to come home to.
But by the time you come back, the cars are
gone, and the cigarette's crushed. But
then there's always the kid down the hall, but
he won't open the door when you come by. At
least he leaves his light on.

And the noise continues upstairs; the
laughter and soft squish of feet against
Persian carpet. And rich cats stay at home
with their wives and play games with your
first editions. Who are these guys who think
because they publish a poem of yours

they have done enough. The misers, leechers,
blood-suckers of the imagination. Creating
nothing (Creation nil in them, but they
think because they participate in "buying"
the avant-garde they have done enough.
Or ordering the advanced record-labels.
Or supporting backing a magazine. Or buying
a book is enough. 35 times its
original price. And that they can
stay home and play diddledy-dat with

that. Who are they, anyway? These pub-
lishers of book, these gourmets
of the avant-garde.

They sit in bars with your friends, and eat their time
away. They leave their wives alone.

                    Road of Straw
        It has been too little judged how much
Ed Marshall's poetry has determined the
verse of the last decade. He directly
influenced the composition by subject matter of Allen
Ginsberg's work, <u>Kaddish</u> and his line
was carried over in "Aunt Rose" and some
of the Gloucester poems by Charles Olson,
namely "The Librarian" ? and Maximus,
vol II.
        In Leave the Word Alone, Ed Marshall
has created the only long spontaneous continuous poem of the
        20th century.
And he was directly influenced by Steve Jonas, under
orders of myself, to a minor degree. But
lesser degrees are not interesting.

And were first given to us in 1955
by Steve Jonas and others, through
the work of Charles Olson, and
Corman produced his program
over the air waves that reached
Robert Creeley's ears in 1949. And
produced Origin, the only little
magazine of the century.

It was Steve Jonas who first presented
to me, and Steve Jonas himself who
first presented to Ed Marshall the
world of Steve Jonas; ~~mental~~
~~hospitals, jails~~ go   the words
of William Carlos Williams, the
technique and rhythms of Ezra
Pound and of the Renaissance Lyrics, The Troubadors, the
     Provencal, Confucius, Thomas Jefferson and Mussolini
          the blast, the vituperative
temper are here carried through to
          an emotion of the highest
lyrical intensity. It is here
that the orders are given to us. And
we must respond to the orders of others or be damned
forever to the streets of Boston. It is here where Steve Jonas
     failed it
the streets of Boston
are damned to us, forever. It is here where Steve Jonas lived*.
* he left the streets of Boston forever by his poetry. "Who does
     he think he is, this time, President Kennedy". He killed
     them, and who must know it, but ourselves?

* And don't try to diddle-daddle with the past, The Stranger
Fruit, as it is.

And it is here in the order of Steve Jonas' poems
that the orders are given.
     And not in the poems, alone. But
by the life also. And life flows
through them and leaves the gutter. Rhode of Straw. And fills
     us up to New Hampshire.
And returns us to our life orders of the   And
     throttles
highest degree; decree. The Tree. The Hanged Man   our

guts. And we love it.
is one of his favorite images and one he has tried to pin
                                on me. It was he who first gave me Tarot
        Deck. a bad one at that.
                                        But leave it at that
** And failed us. By blowing the leaves in the gutter. And not
        leaving them where they fall. In the leaves of the gutter are
        found the lines of this book.

        Steve Jonas first presented
orders to us in the early years of the decade
preceding, the 1950's. And it was
here on the streets of Boston
we first heard Charles Olson, Marshall
received his stimulus, Steve reached
his maturity, and I reamed them
all.
    Steve reached out and found his
maturity there, forever. Gave Marshall
the orders that resulted in the first
magnificent long poem of the century;
and by long poem I do not mean
Maximus, or the Cantos or the Wasteland,
or Venice Poem or From Gloucester
Our of From Idaho Out; but Leave
The Word Alone. Not Kaddish or
Howl; but Leave the World Alone. Nor Anathemate
or In Parenthesis but Leave the Word Alone.
        It should be reprinted again, whole
to show the world as it existed in verse
since 1955. For there was nothing
in verse like it before. And there
has been plenty since. Much of it
ignored but still plenty evident.

Ed Marshall remains totally
ignored since. Steve Jonas seems
totally unrecognized, and I
remain terribly alone, totally ignorant. But it does
not matter. The work has been done.
    The poems remain to me total
evidence of that time. Not that it
is enough to say so.

* Marshall replaced by others under
different guise, but still the object of desire
and hatred, bitterness against life and
the times that produced it.

                II
    Part of the time was Steve Jonas'. We
owe it to him to recognize him as such.
He was the direct influence on Ed
Marshall's life, poetry wise, vide Ed's long
poem <u>Tug of War</u>
unpublished and long since lost. Vide their time together*
    Wherein their
battle is outlined.* We three of   * Are there any
    poems of 1946. Or are
us all spent time in mental asylums.   there
    any of them at all?
along with Joe Dunn, the fourth
    unrecognized partner of one. Dudes Hombres.
                Ranch Types.
The three of them totally
ignored since. And totally ignorant of it.
Totally unrecognized, since. We live on roads of straw,
and look at it burn. We lived on
streets of dream Boston was then 1949, and still is
totally ignorant of, in our imaginations, since, alone and

separate, together.

    It is here in these poems that we
are welded joined together, indissoluable.
For it is here that we are given orders, are vainly ignorant of
    them
the plight of our lives, souls, the plait of it so that the poem
    reveals them to us.

                And these 1500 words,*

                    *these poems show that despite all

our ignorance

                wisdom lives. In our lives. Despite

"Against

                Wisdom As Such"

            (2) For a wisdom is posited there,
as such.

flattery, ignorance. These are the conditions of our lives. It is
    here that
We are judged and found wanting. meet each other
        again on the street of dreams, no regret, totally
ignorant of our lives. And ignorant too. (2) And
a tree, out of which the fourth one blooms,
Joe Dunn or Charles Olson. Who
can say, our father or son. But enough
of this meandering. Meadow We wandered in
Boston Common together then.
See A Series in Ace of Pentacles.
No 5.
Or Ed Marshall's temple wood. I met you
in the Garden, a zoo at
times. Lord, help us. The
curse is lifted, and we are together
again   the moonlight summer in Gloucester, Rockport
    ferries, Chichester apple orchards

That madness. enters
cries out again
into our lives, anew – through
these poems, inviting you
to join them in
our madness. And explore these
meadows as new, these poems anew. Like Louis Zukovsky
called
his book and we do too. To
explore their work is an objectivist's
anthology. And to explore these
poems, these streets and this city

is subjective madness. But to
leave them is even worse. But
enough of sloppy madness. Let
us go on to the utter madness of these
poems. And the city that produced
them. Dictated to against its will.

by Steve Jonas, again in 1952 and onwards. Love, John.

Essay

How does the working man pay for his life? With
his hands. My ancestor, John Laffan, wrote an essay
where he describes the "Morals, Manners and
Miseries of Tenement Houses" in the 19th century. So it
continues today. Still the brute force of others controls
the weakness of the mild, the meek and the tame.
Not that they are without fault or excess, and need

no stricture or restraint; but it is the brute who
domineers over them in most parts of society. It is
their mores that rule the world.

    The world of the intellect or sensibility is excruc-
iated. The poems of Frank O'Hara seem as valid   violet
    crushed against a skyscraper.
testimony in the face of this; All poets do their
work is a triumph of will over those who
seek to dominate their imagination or limit their possibility of
    existing, potentiality
all day. Our father, forgive us our trespasses, we know not
    what we do. <u>as</u> we forgive
        Those who trespass against us.

    I will not open a drawer. But hear it twice. The
way it sounds in his ear and my own and to him and to me. I
    can hear
each creak spring in his bed. Others have
lived in these rooms on either side, but have
moved out quickly, after I have returned
from vacations, or trips. Now we will fight
a duel for life.
    Will the poet win? I do not think so.
    It will teach me to be graceful and swift,
cautious in movements like a caged bird.
    All through this essay, I have wanted to
speak of Randall Jarell the poet, who died this Thursday
    morning,
October 14. But it is too late. He died by lunging
against the side of a speeding car, on a by-
pass in North Carolina, heavily travelled,
not fit for pedestrians.
    As those thundering monsters come charging down

on us from Asia, or Africa, will our re-
volt be any more significant?
                    for creation. It happens every time we lay down
        our pens. The
                                        enemy host moves in.
in any way. I hate all restrictions.
        (last line)
    And yet next door to this room, a man has
moved in, who is "in atheletics" and hammered
on the wall, so hard the plaster fell between the walls, at two
        o'clock this morning, because I typed
wrote on a pillow, so as not to disturb him.
"I'll typewrite on your head," he said.
        when I approached his door about this disturbance.
    This irritates me in every way because I will
be hearing him all the time now – everything I do, he'll hear –
        everything he does, I'll hear.
                his actions designated to
hurt and irritate me in every way possible. He will not open a
drawer but think of me, or slam a door.
"That will serve him right." etc. All the boring
actions he can think of. Which will not be
many. Loud television plays, etc. And I too will be thinking
        of him
in everything I do. It will be so rewarding and humiliating.
He will think of nothing else, I know, and
eventually it will lead him to murder. Me or
someone else's. Usually.
    That is the first noble thought I have had

HAIKU

Yes sir, you got to have your head in the stars.
My heart's in the plunders'. plumber's.

What have you got and
where are you going
that you cant afford to lose some of it
along the way.

I hail myself in the window in the mirror,
and in the window itself, my arm raises.

The smell of his cigar in the room.

There is a music that passes through us, that
is a sign of another spirit than our own –
It is akin to fire, but a mild unseen
fire, that leaps up in a rush, as sun
from a bush. A halo of fire, sunrays
in a cone, rushing as if through Van
Gogh's eyes, off the trees.
   It is a silent fire, that contains music
within it, and gives us a few words to
speak, in a rhythm that is our own, dictated,
   The word mystical is outdated, but how
else to describe it. As soon as a thing is
named, it dies in the imagination.
   It is the unknown that gives power to our
lives. And we go about, continually   A communion

with spirits
living, especially if we decide to live the life
of our dreams. I mean wishes. Desires. Dreams in that way.
We have no other choice but
to accept them as they happen to us. And let them
pass through us as words in the night.
Popular songs do
express the soul of the day. Music
does express the rhythm and longing
of the soul, or psyche, as they call it now.
How hard to learn new words, when
man has carried soul around for two thousand years.

seeking to enchain it.

These words are no more my own, than the clothes I have
on,
I hear them and set them down
They rise to me out of the void, the poetic
imagination.*
as if I had chosen to speak them. This life
is not my own, as if I had chosen to live it.
Sure,   Pity those poor poets who seek to use their own
dilemmas
as a way or means
into the poem. One must be always on
guard against excess. Not the grand
gestures of Whitman, or Blake, or even
Ginsberg, but the petty excess of casual
conversation at the dinner table. These
are the places for communication
with the world of poets. Not the psycho-analyst's
office or couch. Where deep meditation is
forbidden by the presence of another,
this stranger, pryer into the secrets of the

psyche. Allright if it's a friend, but be
on guard.
    It is with your family you can share the
secrets of the past.

We are given life and can throw it away,
We have no choice, once we accept the fact of
And we are given words, and can refuse to hear
Them, can refuse to say those things that pulse through us,
      that is
               in meter of your own voice, your own form.
      We refuse to see things that we want. I love to see
    longing in the face of strangers on the street. It means they
    desire
                     more than they have, they know
    another
                    life outside their own? They dream;
Ah, the sad misery of those who want so
much, who want every bright, glittering
thing that comes their way within their reach. And
why not, as Ray Bremser's mother said to the lawyer. Why
not?

The Living Death
It's hard to believe I'm quite as loaded as I am.
I lie in the coffin of life
My eyes are leaden.

My soul is shook with ancestor's memories,
corridors of fire plague my sight
My body shakes with spasms of light

Shocks shoot through solid as clockwork,
I'm consumed by tentacles of living death,
death living, all about, within. From without

it attacks with a sword in the night.
to cut out my heart from the land of living.
Men, who desert me in this hour of madness.

No hand outstretched, no body laid
all flee as if one had the plague.
Social, ostracized, outcast,
sylvan thief. Who is there to understand
my grief? [illeg] be a leaf shriveled on the tree
Than be this horror that is me.

Shrunken, hollow, gap of teeth.
A picture of Goya rather than Dante.

Harvey
You make love to me in my dreams,
    half-awake, half-asleep
        but still alive in my arms
Oh, hold me again. One minute more

I met a whole lot of men,
and they have come and gone,

Come-Down
I want to go out, go back
to some fabulous dope follow through the streets.
some star to track across the wilderness of space,

I want excitement, romance, adventure,
and danger, I want seas at night
and summer mists of Los Angeles,
pines of Black mountain, new moons, new songs,
new girls, night-clubs, opening doors, sharp clothes
glittering in neon lights, concrete stained with rain,

newspapers gathering wind on Main Street, broad thoroughfare,
parks stained with Autumn, ponds, marble sculptures in Rome,
airplanes, terminals, bus stations, anywhere the light is on
all night, I want to go,

be out, there with the jazz, jostling through crowds, on the
    way to concerts,
ballet, opening nights, subway rides, box seats,
orchestra rows, Madison Square Garden, Central Park in
    August
boat rides, tickets torn in two, lovers' mouths against mine

I want late night parties, Garbo against windows, terraces
opening out on gardens, fountains, Christmas, midnight
    movies,
restaurants, models, ankle-straps, costumes, Klieg lights

I want paintings, and painters, good food, rare wines, oceans
at my disposal, Joanne Kyger, poets reading to small audiences,
I want books, finely printed, and bookstores open at Twilight
                in New York, or Big Sur

fire-places, soprano voices and bear rugs over bare flesh,
stone-houses, lonely rides, maryuane to the moon,
old friends, and the death that is not hard in dying,

but this life that is devoid of the eternal I want more of,
Speed, music, excitement.

        It is the act of the lover
Smothering your face with kisses,
is what I think of, when I come

except my face is yours,
and mine also that girl, whom you kiss –

It is a mystery. How I can be
two places at once

Only my beloved, it is you, you
over again, in my dreams

I see, with the full lips,
and mouth, straining to kiss.

2.
I have not made it clear.
I see you, at the moment of

orgasm, straining to kiss
some unknown object

some nothing, just kissing

And I am brought to bear
at the moment of climax,

how I would like to share
that agony.

No girl, no man, nothing,
just kissing

over and over again
this moment of love

what does not exist,
except the act, itself,

3. This is not a good enough poem.
    The face of the beloved shines through

The cloud of orgasm; and what I want to say is
he does not kiss anything, but is just kissing

over and over again, because that is what he was meant to
do.

I don't know what I'm going to do for supper,
We don't have nothing to eat.
Just a dead leaf past the window –

HAMMOCKS

It don't matter to me whether you do or dont
It just matters to me whether you will or wont.

Oh God, just to have this room, these books, this
roof over my head, men
in my life, my name in books – I want this ecstasy
to go on forever.
    I have nothing to say but holy worship of the gifts
that are mine, that have been given me to use, -- this
    investigation
of place

Candles in the daylight; don't put them out.

Love is a word on the page, – stained with sperm,

Love is a word on the page, stained with sperm – orgasm.
Love is dropping off my arm, now.
Love is time and you coming back.

Love is a trick in the night.
Love is dull, without you.
Love is unattainable.

Love is within me, never found but belly to belly
Love is the closing of a door, with a friend behind it.
Love is shit on your hands.

The Rooming House
for John

I dont want to work,
I want to lie down
and rest for the rest
of my life. No cig-
arettes. I can't do it,
work. Tijuana Brass
plays up the hall. That ass
who plays it. Fat-assed.

His cheeks have fallen,
Ed Dorn would say.
The poem falls too, at these
distractions.

The Rooming House (Second Version)
for John

I dont want to work.
I want to lie down
and rest for the rest
of my life. Isnt that
what the Muse means?
by the root of her word,
to think, remember. mou-
tai, from the pre-Hellen-
ic Greek. Ah God, it's good
to know something.

THE BOARDING HOUSE
Night, and a long day's weeping,
the sheets stained with excrement, candles leaping
at the window, steam pipes hiss,
a goblet filled with piss.

Night, and a long day's weeping,
the bronze athletes stalk corridors,

television plays under the doors,
fat asses, full glasses, the only girl in the place
        walks with a cane, leaping

Night, and a long day's weeping.
A mouthful of teeth gone, dinner done, yet
The heart is not full, empty in bed alone, the boarding house
closes its doors and lets out no small figure
        on rain-washed streets, weeping.

Lets no small figure out to the moon on rain-washed streets,
    weeping
        with its doors closed,

A Short Story

John's a slattern from the middle-classes,
in his old wrapper,
half-man, half-woman.

his feet bare, caked with dirt.
but still some elegance remains, from another century.

Ancestor was John Laffan, a sheriff under Elizabeth
the time of Irish rebellion, Tipperary
and another was one of the principal men in Wexford
James Laffan. And old family dating back to the Norman
        conquerors

But still one lost in poverty and ignorance now.
No knowledge of his heritage left, in the small room
        where he lived
fenced in by the back wall of one of those squat white buildings

plate glass in front, cinder blocks in back, two stories high
that so dominate the landscape of provincial cities, cut off
from the metropolis, but still close enough to know one exists.

So is Buffalo close enough to New York, but not close enough
    to be of any use.
He could not accept it as a half-way measure. Nor could he
    accept himself.

Lying as he was, in the half-light of taking and giving, yet not
    having enough
to do either, simply being

    And his body began to rot because of this equalization,
    this void
where excess and plenty were forbidden, where denial and
    want were
                    forbidden

where waiting alone is all. And even that dies, in the morning
light, dull and grey, as it was, that filtered in over the
roof of this dull, grey building, squat, two stories
high, in the back of a parking lot, his windows
two inches from that wall.

    He tried to practice remembering, but that was gone, too
exhausted by youth. He tried to listen to his neighbors, but
    they
were going for the holiday. Thanksgiving Eve. November
24, 1964. Still better than last year, wasn't it? When
he was stuck home, in his parent's house, family as they
were, and all he had in the world, now suddenly he thought,
this is all in the world, I have. This dull light, this
footsteps on the ceiling of his last neighbors, preparing
to leave; the dull roaring of highway traffic, all speeding

to destinations never known. Let them join in. Let
all come down in one great gust of breath, he said.

But nothing stirred. Only the hiss of steam from
the radiator pipes. He could go downtown. He
could go to a movie. Lots were looking for love, lost souls
    wandering, on a
day such as this, when the excess and intimacy of
family life turned them out, to seek love:
on their own terms. But such derelicts of the
heart and soul; he already knew this. He must fight against
them. He could see himself later in the day wandering
theatre corridors, spending what little money
he had, and ending up the day later in some still
bar, where no music played, but on juke boxes
loud and clear and violent, of the search of the soul,
against them, family-minions in or out of love.

His neighbors had gone. The rooms were quiet. Only
as I say, the hissing from steam pipes radiated thru
the day. He reminded him of far away, some vague
landscape, he could not tell where, not even fully
realized, not even recognized; Niagara Falls, it
became because that was near at hand. But it was not
that. It was more than that. Some psychic chamber
of the soul, where waters flowed, where exhaustion
wearied them, some spa of the Black Forest, where men
became young and men regained the beauty lost to them

psyche   Even his handwriting changed, as he thought about
    this,
(he had been writing in his journal) you probably noticed this,
some Guinevere with golden waist clasp, some Isolde came to
    mind, some
Brunhilde of times past with black trees behind her

stalks of trunks, smooth as black hands, or fingers be-
hind her. Some confusion had gone. Some
beauty had been returned to him. He could go now
on the street, singing as of yore. Visit the
University Plaza, by foot, eat.
In the rain-drizzled streets.
 Alright, he was not in the Black Forest.
He would escape to there. Not now, but forever
he would go there. His handwriting changed
again as he thought of this. Those black
trees, the green grass beneath them sparkling
with silver dew, and presided over by a golden-haired maiden
 who
dressed in white gown leaned over
and said, I love you over again and again.
 Who did not weep, but left her tears? on
the grass, or was that dew Duncan speaks of, who ran
her fingers to the sides of her hair, distractedly,
which flowed in great curls on her shoulders,
and she smiled with white teeth between them, red lips like
 some
Ziegfeld Follies girl of the past. But the Ziegfeld
Follies girl only imitated her, as I do in my white
wrapper, trimmed with brown, John thought as
the day went down into darkness before it even
begun.   in plate glass and neon lights, even in
 Rome where most all Bostonians go,
 sooner or later.

 II As Everywhere Else
 The traffic in the city of Boston has steadily increased; they
 have torn down
the West End, they have torn down Scollay Square;
and nearly all of Copley Square, making

145

thoroughfares out of them and parking lots. Urban renewal,
they call it. Erecting insurance companies, garages and
They have put in along the broad avenues. so many autos no
    one can go out in the
               daytime anymore.
They put night-clubs, Peter Pan
Gone the old, elegant hotels, the basement underground
    cafeterias
The walk-in, jazz clubs and strip atheneums, all-night
              movies,
          Boyston and Essex: The Silver Dollar!
              all gone.
        old haunts of these poems.
They have become bombs to blow up in the face of the future:
    BLAST.
They have become the future; and also emblems of the past
    we live in.
  Queen's Row is no more. Those bricks on Arlington Street,
    known the world over
now moulder in the city sun, the Queen's Rosary, once counted
    the button on a sailor's fly,
is no more. 13 in all. Instead retreated to the men's room,
             where for the price of a dime,
                you can purchase a flea.
Beacon Hill is no more, with its expensive apartments on all
    sides.
          The Lincolnshire where Eugene O'Neill
          died now a Nurses Home.
       The North End holds its own, but the gangsterism
present there prevents a Kind inhabitation.
  What is left? The South End. Where the Poet lives. Boston
    has no
East End, tho there is an East Boston, only the desperate go
    there.
  It is here in the South End the Poet plys his trade. Here the

outcasts
of the old times live.   But Jan Balas still stumbles
    through the streets at dawn.

No longer Billie Holiday at the Savoy. No longer
Malcolm X at Mass Avenue, The Roseland Ballroom,
                instead score at the pharmacy on Huntington
    Avenue but that's burnt down
                                    now, I bet, too.
no   longer   Tremont   and   Boylston   for   Billy   Donahue.
    They've gone to Roxbury.
He's gone underground too, to the Navy Yard. I thought that
    was Roger Weber's
Tramping ground – Anyway here is Steve Jonas, here is the
    language he lives by,
here is the city he lives in, here are the gods he lives from, the
    poets he lives out,
and the painters he lives with. Here is the poetry he makes live.

                The Anticipation of Youth
    Imagination has worn out. I can do no more than see what's
in front of me, set up what's straight. Sleep is impossible.
I am too tired for that. And the mind has worn down to thick
grooves in the record that repeat and repeats itself.
I long for adventure as of old. On street-corners, where
the haven of the heart is fulfilled. But it is no dice. I am too
        tired to
make the journey. My liver hurts constantly. A pressure
against the sides that bloats with water unpassed through
the bowels. Too tired to eat. To rise to the occasion. I feel like
an old man.

Poetry does not desert me. The rain still makes a melody on the street. But when the ink in this pen runs out, I will not get up to fill it. Good bye.

    Of course when one is dissatisfied with the present, one
        takes to
reminiscing. But I hesitate to do so, having spent
the last years of the twenties – 1961 – 1962, and
1963-1964 – 27 and 28 – 29 and 30 doing
this. I remember the beat streets of San Francisco,
Grant Avenue with its open stalls of fruit and
vegetables, hardly ever bought for lack of money and
the open stalls of Avenue C in New York City, when the
Lower East Side began to bloom – and one shopped there,
from the Jewish merchants rather than the Chinese
ones of San Francisco. "Now all is gone, gone is the
rapture I knew so well."
    Billie Holiday ushered in my youth, when I
I was 12, 1946 – and she sang on Commodore Records,
"Strange Fruit" and she ushered it out when she
died in New York, July 19th 1959 thirteen years
later. I met her once at the High Hat in Boston when I was 21.
    and heard her many times afterwards
    in Boston and San Francisco.

    She had a great quality to her voice in that she never seemed
        aware of what the audience was thinking of her, tho I
        remember, was totally absorbed in what she was doing,
        a passion for
concentration, derived or gained, probably from the junk she
        was using.

on a record, made for Recording Industries Corporation of
America, at Storyville in Boston 1959, year or so before her
    death, when she seemed so aware

of what the audience was thinking, how bitchy she became
at their inattention, the drunks calling her name, etc., their
favorite requests,

Anyway she was 25 when I was first born on earth, and
I was 25 when she left it. Strange coincide. Some goddess
of youth. This world-weary woman who turned her dreams
to ashes. As I have become of her, enamored of her
ashes on the voice I was asking of her. That doesn't
make any sense, her sense to me, when I should be out on
the street, living her life, blowing some colored cock. But
that is not the answer.

Get back the compassion and wisdom. lost with
youth, left of her, get it back, before it is too late.

The envy and drive she had to sing of love, I must
speak, of her. My goddess of youth. Remembered of her
now that youth is gone, is lost to me, I say, "as if
all youth were gone. Credit Robert Duncan with maintaining
what youth and love I have, gone with her

Charles Olson with maintaining it. But I dont want
this to be a paean of love to memory past. I want
to go out and find it. And I will.

Well, I found love and what is it, a stranger's kiss. Can be
more than re-union with a lost friend.
For the friend produces a different kind of
excitement, a more conscious one. While the kiss of a
stranger combines with excitement and releases
a loneliness in the soul that is imperative. "Loosens
the limbs" Hesiod would say of Aphrodite. And that is just
        where
I feel it the most, in the back of the legs and all through them,
        that delicious bath of the senses,
the tactile ones that produces a quietude that
is rare and not easily found, or come by. It is

necessary if the soul is to rest in peace.
 The soul is out-dated. I must use the new
word, which is only a return to the <u>oldest</u> word. Psyche.
I must write new poems. I must anticipate comfort,

even if it is not here. The anticipation of youth. I must
not grow old or bitter, and give up hope. Of
what? Youth returning to me, but it has not left.
 I must find the new key to words. I must
produce more. I must be the new Rimbaud,
and not die at 37, nor Hart Crane, either. but set the record
 straight,
new words to music, the key to existence.
 I must not be afraid to be humiliated, by
these people here. I must continue on my way.
new journey to oblivion, paradise in the jungle,
the savage that America has become.
 I must set down how difficult it is for me, to
make sense, how for every word set down, there is
a void waiting for me, a possibility of contradiction.
This is not dictation. There can be contradiction.
 I must persevere in my youth, and guide the foot-
steps of the young toward truth, in my ignorance.

I must fight for the right word, the exact sentence, the
precise meaning, I must have meaning.
I must wait for the right word. I must read more.
And compose poems, listen carefully.
I call upon the Muses, "veiled in mist". I must not
forget them. I must have nothing to do with ignorance.

 And writing that, I forgot next what I had to say. I must
write carefully, form my letters with more skill, prac-
tice and learn how to develop the art of poetry.
 I must observe its disciplines. Clear my mind,

get plenty of sleep, eat well, keep me in shape as I have tried
    the way of abandon
                        in opposition to them,
                            destroyers of
poetry by
their "order," which
is not order at all,
but doubt and
convention.
so the word may "always" pass through my brain and ears,
    andI be in fit form to receive it. A receptacle for that
most precious of all instruments, poetry, for registering
the universe with more skill, care and feeling
than any other art, or instrument. Telescope or not.
I can see the star glitter on this previous page,

more bright than any mechanical eye. Silver it
shines there where no camera could catch it.
The music of this dance registers the flash
more clearly than any cold ear could hear it.
So it goes and has become in these words, by the uttering
                        of them
a more precious gem than in any other diadem.
An instant flash, more splashy, it is not just by rhyme
we do it, but no other eye could see it, no other time
    but the art of poetry could hold it for the instant and that
    it is,
        in the kiss of words against each other.
            Oh Mother memory, may it go on forever.
            May we learn the words for the new music.
                May you teach them to us.
            May we get a good night's sleep.
            May we rest in your bosom eternal.
                May our meaning be precise.

151

SOLUTION

Barbarians straddle the throne.
Old loves of the past stare from vacant picture frames.
Lights shine alone in the closet.

Dull lines of poetry stride across each page.
Night is here, but where
are the muses?
the dreams of yesteryear.

Gone asleep on the plain, gone the jazz,
gone the dull refrain
of pain upon each page.

I pass before the looking glass,
past thirty, hoping to recall
what I missed by poverty.

But each instant shines in its own
minute reflection of life, not enough
to say I missed this, I wanted that.

I tried every trick possible to gain the crown.
Barbarians straddle the throne.

Madness took away the prize. I struggle now
to retain what fragments of mind are left, what gain
there is from the prize that is the poem,

There is none. I abandon no instant, but wish
there were more upon the page. That friends
would not write and say Fame is in the making
It is the poem I make.

Madness struggles for the hand that writes this page
Not madness in the old sense, the madness of chaos w/o
clarity, the madness of confusion without calm, or care.

I put out my cigarette upon the mirror. And look upon my
    hand
as the old guard of treason, of age without withering.
It rejuvenates before my eyes.

The strain goes. The muscles relax. The bulge of nerves
against the skin recoil, liquid flows back to its original source,
the heart.

The barbarians do not reach this frontier.

The mind does not relax before their onslaught.
Their only salvation.

Here the instants are preserved. Time is gone,
yes, but stays here eternal in the poem.
Fragments are shored against the ruin
that is time, that does not pass, but takes away.
I cannot sleep. There is no sleep without heroin.

    (Two weeks previous to previous entry)

<u>Last Entry</u>

My mind is coming back slowly, I can tell. The inner
voices make sense now. They no longer tell me to do ir-
relevant things or contradict each other.

    I like writing better with a free-flowing pen.
Its spirit seems to run freer and with more spirit.

Of course, when one pain decreases, another increases.
Now the pain in my head increases, from sinus.
It is concentrated mainly over the right eye.
    How good it is to talk again and make sense.

The mind is a structure that can be blasted a-
part, into a thousand bits, all of them not making
sense except in isolated fragments, though brilliant
                        still frustrating to the creative mind which
        is trying
                        to communicate itself in sentences more
        complex
                    than statements of help or longing or dismay.

                no inter-relationship at all, it is
the mind's job
how to build that relation back, call it sanity
When it coheres, when these fragments congeal, when there is
        a memory or past, when
the structure holds, when a sentence can be
more than a beginning and an end, one can take a chance and
                leap out, not compulsively as before, but with more
        surety, when there is rhyme in the mind's question,
                    not confusion or chaos, the
                        handwriting holds, unless
                        one wants it to go (its springs
                            from reading, I think)
                    and talking with friends, wise men, gods, saints,
        poets, ah yes not egos
when one is sure of himself, not interrupted by a thousand
contradictions or possibilities; one can make style out of
        himself when one is led not by distraction
however compulsive that may be. The
rest is silence. And frightening to behold in a writer.
                    Ah well,

the frenzy ~~on this page, it takes to~~ it takes to communicate a
   ~~belief~~ ~~knowledge~~
              that thought.

              Love,
                 John Wieners
                 November 28, 1965
                 4AM – Sunday
                 Morning

No birds as sweet.   2.

There is a human quality to your walk
like a giant bird come to rest on earth for a little while
Oh God, if you walk out of my life. Walk back

A HOUSE IN THE WOODS—
MOTHS AT THE WINDOW

Soon up the gravel path. ~~Outside~~ the stones —
without a phone, with only a voice to reach the stars
Glow in the afternoon, ~~fire fly~~ fire fly, on the couch

of my dreams, come true. ~~Lioness of the cub hunt~~
                    3,

Blood-root in your hand, as you walk back
in this room of the dream and shadow,
the child and maiden — goddess in one.
At the ends of the earth — Annisquam.

John Wieners
    gift of Panna Grady
    New York City
    April 24th 1966

    Sunday

Noted Gloucester June 29th, 1966   Wednesday
                        Evening
with the rail falling outside on the trees,
And love falling in our hearts,
May it rise again.
May it hoot in the night like the train
                        whistle,
like the horned owl, The snapping Turtle

May we become one again and dwell in our hearts
        as we dwell in Thee,
Lord sleeping in the night, upstairs—

        A House in the Woods – Moths at the Window
            Plan of Book
First Meeting March 17th – 1965
Return – The Five Spot – 2 days at The Dakota
                    March [illeg]
Return to Buffalo – Spring Arts Festival

First trip to Gloucester – The Motel
Princeton – April 24th – Sunday dinner w/ Howard Hart
　　　　　Monday dinner with Kenward Elmslie &
　　　　　　　　Gerrit Lansing
Second Visit to The Dakota – Cote Basque – The Drake
　　　　　　　　Hotel
May 15th (1966) – Conceive child　　　　　(Shepherd's)
Leave for Gloucester – May 17th
Buffalo　Return May 20th – 1966
　　　　Part Two　　June 1st –
Gloucester I (Panna's Arrival – Margo Leave)
Return to Milton　　June 14th
Sale of The Dakota
Gloucester II (Irving and Dave)　June 15th –
　　　　　Father's Day in Boston　June 19th
Return to New York – Abortion?
Sister's Wedding　　　　June 26th
　　　Monday Party in Gloucester
[illeg]hearts　　Tuesday Meeting with Charles and Ralph Maud
　　　　Wednesday　– Return
Sunday　　Parting –　　　　with Ralph Maud –
Abortion July 5th – 1966 – (Tuesday Night with Charles.
　　3PM
Return　July 12th – July 11th – House-Cleaning

　Friday the News –
　Saturday – Alone Together

To Bacchus

June 1

Panna arriving today, Going down to open bottle of Tattinger
Champagne. Lucky me, with Keys to front door hang-
ing out of breast pocket,   [illeg]   my heart. Ah –
    Dave Haselwood has become a tulip on my shelf,
printing <u>Hotel Wentley</u> poems now, for the third time.

June 1966 – an eight year cycle since they were
first written.
June 6th – Invitation – Invocation to Spring – Past
                    over a Summer
    Our time here is enchanted. What more is there to say?
    The flowers are perfect. They do not die.

    Love is endless in the afternoon
    midwinter suns
                descend on the woods

        Stars bloom over our heads

    Ah, descend again sweet love. Pick sweet wines.
    out of the air.
Make bouquets to wake me in the morning. Run cool hands
    over my back.   Descend, sweet love.

    Make new again these woods. Unwreath
    the secrets of your arms, your voice

    a melody so rare there is nothing to compare
    with it. Brandy in the blood is not so hot

Nor birds as sweet
                2.

There is a human quality to your walk

like a great bird come to rest on earth a little while.
Oh God, if you walk out of my life. Walk back

soon up the gravel path. Crunch over the stones ¾
without a phone, with only a voice to reach the stars.
Glow in the afternoon, fire fly, on the couch—

of my dreams, come true.

3.

Blood-root in your hand, as you walk back
in this room – of the dream and shadow,
the child and maiden – goddess in one.
At the ends of the earth – Annisquam.

• 7

Love has come to our house. In the woods
after the rain through the trees,
        with the last singing of birds at twilight.

Fin-de-siècle.

    The century matters not,

the music matters more

    That is neither heaven or earth,

but the feet of a child upon the stairs.

2.

Sucking her milk,
asking, where are you?Crawling on the bed,
playing with cigarettes,
Being a pest, but still here—
asking please in a childish voice
and pink dress
                    3.

The night turns dark,
The woman in the kitchen playing with pots & pans,
        pregnant.
The suburban images fade,

            all rises
        in a cacophony of sounds
That herald another night on the farm,
            our Swiss chalet
                    carved out of stone
            from Gloucester quarries.

            Great Life Is
[. . .]
            She said this morning on the stairs
as I whispered her name thru the railing.
    "Um".   "Um".   "Um," we communicated but now
the afternoon is here, birds sing above the lawn,
time slips by on wingèd feet, and music plays in the kitchen.
    The first LSD novel, that is what this is going to be. 500
    words
                    a day.

To record our love affair, whatever that is.

    She slipped into the living room, while I was writing this,
      yet
her shadow does not fall against the wall, but I know it.

   The clink of cups in the kitchen, recording of phenomenology
It is not enough, but a record is.

    Of our times together, water rushing in the sink,
The rub of genitals against the hand, the empty stomach
which we hope she will fill, but it is not necessary.

    We continue without it. With that poise and calm
writers have, which women see, and envy it. That
is what she saw when she slipped into the living room just
      now,
but I do not have breakfast, and wish I did. As I do not know
I can continue without it.

    No juice has been offered, no kind word extended.
Only "Um". "Um," "Um" and Great Life Is.

    Said at the top of the stairs, in the morning
or afternoon, or early evening, I cannot tell which.

    But that's all right. Let her go. I don't need it.

    She has work to do, or thinks she does.

    Just as I do.

    But I need her, in this house, at this time, moving thru
the rooms like show business, satisfying the minds of men.
        2.

    It's a grey day, And we have been to Boston. Rode the
Swan Boats of the Public Garden, in the morning. Ate
breakfast at Sharaf's. Took a ride downtown And
a train home to the North Shore, and are now together in
this house, waiting for the next move.

    I am happy in this house.

    Ella slams the door and comes in. She is Panna's
child, three years old last Sunday, and she was with us

on our trip to Boston this morning. She has been with us
on many trips. New York, Buffalo, Princeton, Gloucester.
Not really, but there nonetheless. Now she is gone, out the
    door.
Collecting faggots for the fire.
         3.

   You'd think Panna would be happy here in this house with
    me. That
we were in the woods and together

       To Panna
Everytime I close my eyes,   I see your face
Smiling   within the light,   behind my lids.

     For my sister's wedding at 40

Pierced with a miniature electric track
on which no trains run,
our back against the wall,
This shock treatment does not cure

As it's supposed to,
only reduces sustained intellectual effort,
and turns poets into dogs.
Ah Doctor Cassidy,

I hope you're satisfied

with the 900 dollars my parents
                          to pay you
borrowed from the bank (and paid back) but not by.

only now to borrow back to paint the house with

For my sister's wedding at 40.

We have a flame within us, I told Charles

All my old foes turned friends,
Why, because I entered the circle of the damned,
and escaped with a halo around my head,
which burns now with the bright glow of electricity.

I want the frim-fram sauce
& the oysterate wishefifer on the side.

Dont want eggs & bacon
Now I may be mistaken

Five will get you ten.

Drinkin Lonely Wine

When you're used to taxicabs,
you can't take buses –
        & champagne & caviar

You can't switch hamburgers with relish
I am a product of the times
in <u>country houses</u> --_ with rich heiresses and poor parents
w/out tenement walls. How can I
go back to dreamin when reality's has become

heaven. Oh roses blooming in the afternoon,

shadows on oriental rugs –

phonograph records,

[edge torn out] rosé wines, – rings of diamond,

        you should last forever
ah belles –   dreaming in the afternoon
        bring me back to paradise.

I need no empty afterglow now

when women with long legs walked thru the room

Trailing their legs like swans.

and heavy breasts
        hair of coronets & diamonds
        ah Panna
take up the cudgel, now

and beat my brains in
before I go any further.

Your dreams destroy me
        "golden girl of the twenties,
          Ginger Rogers.

       "purchasing value out of nowhere."
      Olson said on the porch
You poets dream on

And find where the path leads you

An empty face in a glass

That is not so full anywhere else.

        Looking for you
          Since you're gone.

     Chapoutier & Cie CAVEL

Vin rosé
is so clear in the afternoon light

What difference does it make
if my heart is broken in two & runs red
It is the same with her
on her way to New York with our unborn child in her belly
   [. . .]

It does not matter if his blood runs red

in the afternoon,

>> This wine is pink

and consoles me.

Brandy,   -
                il seura seul ma fatigué   -
its not brain candy,
nor nose either,
but it's a breather,
you can't deny it.

Let's face it,
drink it and see.
You'll get a breeze—,
and a freeze, too.
That's all you do, —

sip it and see—
with chocolate –
you'll not be isolate any longer.
You'll get stronger –
You'll agree
That's all there is to it.
Ask Napoleon,

ask Courvosier,
ask Remy Martin.
They all brew it

And knew it, too
in their own time.
Pardon this odd rhyme —
but it's the only way I can climb
                    lady
to heaven, where the brandy is

In your arms, brandy
My girl, my sweet.
        You are so neat.
The birds descend —
to listen to your voice —
when I drink brandy
in the afternoon, alone.

No knock sounds at the door
and night is descending on the lawn outside.

Why should lovers part?

Misericorde – Edith Piaf sings.

But at least I have a phonograph to listen to it, and
I have known the love of a woman – it is not over yet
They can't take that away from me – no, it is not over yet
nor is our love. We are in new health, and we shall
have this child together. There is nothing to do about it

This is a novel of love. Charles would not deny it. Even if I
    have to get drunk

to write it or be in pain. Who would believe it? That the most
    notorious faggot
of our times would fall in love with the best most beautiful
    woman, after a West Indian and
an Anglo-Saxon Yankee middle class bourgeois. Now a wealthy
Connecticut heiress. It does not seem fair to inflict such
    extremes upon one man

not to mention the numerous Jews I have been
enchanted by, and the numerous witches
I have enchanted with; no, it does not seem fair,
and the rich men I have held dear, and the poets
I have heard as divine. No, the gods do not
seem to do justice – and yet they have descended
as living men and I have welcomed – known them – all –
pledged myself to them from the beginning –
Now I am rid of this writing, and can rise again
to the tasks of this day – the rain – 5AM. That is
approaching. – and the dust that is accumulating –
and the dinner that has to be cooked.

Panna's Return from New York

      moves
As the field mouse runs over tiles,
return love to our house,
    as rain falls
on the trees, truss up my beloved,
for eternity in my arms.

As her child sleeps in the upstairs bedroom
may our love live forever in our hearts,
may she give herself to me in the night
and trust the love I hold

in my arms to her now.

As she cooks in the kitchen

as she runs water for the meal

while the man upstairs sleeps in the guest room
with our love between his hands.

May this pain lift off, may it go away
and not come again. May she ~~love me~~ live forever.

as I got out now to help her lift the yellow table

off the kitchen floor onto the living room and

and prepare to meet the guests we have not invited

Love and trust.   June 29th 1966

To Panna

Whose creation this is,
I don't know.

Or how the stars came to be above,

I don't know.

But that there is love,
and I care to share it with you

I do know now

Love, true love

what creation this is.

Abortion

She's decided to do it. Out in the kitchen now with Ralph
    Maud,
        be
How can I not use the personal?

            When the rain drops from trees,
in the wind when there is no rain.

I can stand this. Let them make love. I'd much rather stay
    home.

You know, Ella's here.   And love is here in my heart.
No matter what they do to it. I'm not cutting any child out of
    my belly.

She is. Let her. The ages will judge her.

How can I rise to the occasion and still keep my manhood
There is no possible way of doing it.

Let them practice their murderous ways. They are used to it.

The murderer and the vampire. They have killed one poet
after another. Lorca. Spicer. The dead do not remember the
 living. The living do not remember the dead. Only as they
 see them. Beloved Poets. And they are part of the living.
        It is all right. Let them do it.

I never wanted success. I never wanted fame: I wanted success
 in new adventures.

I wanted jubilation. I wanted new words for these things.

I wanted to raise my flag for poetry.

And they have pulled it down. Tattered and rumpled. Let
 them.

 It is still flying somewhere.

     I cannot leave her. I cannot even write.

I can do nothing but sit and brood.

    The wine sits in the sunlight, turning to vinegar

Whey use to quell sensuous women. Whey use to douche with

    And kill unborn babies.

Oh the blood of the world is upon my hands. The murder of innocent

women

is perpetuated by their daughters. The womb of the living

is torn open

to expell the dead, while they still have the breath of life within them

Thomas is destroyed. Light fled. How can I let this woman do this?

When they have burnt out my brains, I let them expell my child

from its womb.

Not hers, but my womb now. I am sick on the taste of my tongue. I am sick of the act I am doing. Perpetuated upon the womb.

I have cast my seed upon the wind.

"Cast thy bread upon the waters", the old monument of an angel throwing bread to the winds said in the Public Gardens at the corner of Arlington Street, "for thou shalt find it after many days."

And now they have taken my bread, so short-lived in its infancy

And cast it upon the waters of the world.

Oh God, fate is upon us. I shall not commit suicide. I shall not be

Sylvia Plath

and put my head in the oven. These are not real
people.

       They can go to a festival tonight and pretend
nothing is hopping.

           Fiesta de San Pietro in Gloucester, Mass.

      For thy name is Peter and upon this rock I shall
build my Church.

Oh Petra.   Sunday Morning

She thinks I will do her violence. I will not. She is preparing
my meal. I dont want to eat it but will – have to. [illeg].

  Every $\left\{\vphantom{x}\right.$ Where is the beauty I need to sustain the
wickedness of our ways?

      Then she is going to Fiesta with Ralph
                Maud.

And watch the Statue of Saint Peter carried through the streets
of the town,

      with dollar bills pinned to his gown.

    And I wanted to call my child Peter.
[. . .]

To Bud Powell and Fats Navarro
("Fat Girl")

Alcohol doesn't ease the pain,
nor dope does,
maybe music if it evokes love,
~~but I doubt it~~.

You could with that child in your belly,
but that is over now,
possibly friends but they are gone.

The record's over, play another –
see the sunlight through the window,
hear the trumpet, drink Alsace wine –
it will not bring you back,

gone to New York, and my cock stinging.

My child swinging for a few more days.
Maybe tomorrow they can get you in –
and then, the knife

Dom Perignon
1959

One of us is going to die,
          I dont know which

champagne and cake on the balcony

geraniums new-planted under the moon,

under the moon on the coast,

        The geraniums,
       Their faces freshly painted
          glow/ in the shore, also of the wall

     with a luminous red I have never seen before –

– at twilight –

         The sky grey –

    but the geraniums

        vibrous
  than the firefly

different than the centre to

    Shubert's Last Songs,

      fringed Gentians
   different [illeg]
    of Lawrence.

  Only you, geraniums
       of the moon.
    Our Unborn Child

A butterfly inside you died

in my dream. It had orange wings

Billie Holiday. She had wings, too.

Sang to her man on trumpet,
Joe Guy, 1946. Hollywood Bowl

not the thousands who heard
        listened to her
    My pain is real. I tell you I mean it.

The applause means nothing. But could
            live without it.

Where is the dream I bore within her. Fell over on the floor
                crucified   and died.
Folded those orange and black wings, that moth did.
    Crumpled Collapsed on the floor
        like a range of mountains
us no more in the dawn or afternoon

        where I dreamed him.

May 15th.   (She lived off love)
                Cherry

and it is all over

Oh lover if you only could sing as this trumpet
man does, I would love you forever.
But it is over,
you could never
        give yourself as this man,
So farewell, let you go –

to Bill Burroughs, and who –

ever wants you,

I am through.

Mahler
Lieder Eines Fahrenden Gesellen

There is no wickedness, I do not want
    black magic or
To invoke the devil
commit sacrilege   rather appease the gods

who create shining in the night
            and let a child

    I will sing songs to him like Brahms or August von Platen.
Please god, do this for me. Holy, holy —
in the moon, on the moon, one more time,
shine on us and release this dream to waking.
Let no tears fall. Panna get out of the hospital.

Get up out of the bed and walk to the door. Get your clothes
and go into the streets. See the city with our child in
                        your belly.
It will not hurt. It is only the moon that hurts you.
                    It will pass.
Pass by that door marked death and you will live forever
                in your son.

In the Darkness

It's a mistake to assume love,
where none exists
    We create within our hearts
   a worthy object.   for ourselves alone.
Out of
Others may share it and enter that sacred glow,

but it is a matter of our caring alone.

We want something
and build accordingly,
but foolish to believe
it will be there when we need it the most.

Alone on a hospital bed, say –
or in jail. I have been in The Hotel Dixie
where no one cared – alone, among thousands– still, within the
    family breast,
it lives, and with friends,

                There burns
a like recognition of the eyes.

        I have built
a fire now to warm me through these summer days.

I only hope you come back soon

        to warm your hands

        at its dull blaze.

HIATUS

Rest in the dream, that's all I can do.
Hear bells tinkle on the grass
and birds sing.

Smoke in bed,
and wait for your return
all morning long.

Sit on silk pillows
worked with peacock designs
and golden swans.
Write poems
before a yellow table
in the dawn all morning long.
Hear grass rustle in the yard,
and trees blow.
See Mrs. Coyle the landlady
cut milk weed drunkenly
and then do three days' dishes
in the sink
all morning long.

See her pass before the dragon lilies,
lock the foundry shed,
each single simple event invested with divinity
and then the pause
when no words come
for the rest of the morning

July 5th 1966

I said to her this afternoon. Don't go to the hospital.
Don't kill what has never lived. I beg you.

On my knees. Soren Agenoux. Some people
are better off never born.

Be-
                smirch with kisses
                        my brow.
        [← Call me callous,
        cold and low,
                indifferent to you now.

                Satyrs and Nymphs
Titanic I love you as much
                as I do anyone else in the world.
The birds, trees.
I equate you with these. These   Thank you.
Marlene Dietrich, no more than that.

Moody's Mood for love.
                Billie's Bounce//
2.
Dancing in the morning
                alone
                        out to the porch
not on my knees, as yesterday
                singing the Psalms
to keep our child in your belly.
                Oh Billie

pray for me

that she

deliver this child today
                and not kill it

as we have killed so many in our lives.

How the trees rustle,
The flute blow –
                Pan rests on the lawn
for the next attack, the next angel
                        to wander
down the road, and ask, is this road open?

It is, for love always

3.
"to make these feelings evident is the work of an artist."

Hearing old jazz blow.
It seems a bird got caught in our machine.
Oh archer, skill my hands,
shoot this arrow
        close to her lands,
~~that I might be entwined in her life~~

        ~~from now on,~~
~~this moment pledge to her my love,~~

        ~~my hope~~

~~that our lives be never ending now~~.

~~Engaged as we are in this eternal voyage~~.

That our lives be intertwined as wings on the air

(before the phantom stranger arrives)

to take her away in the form of death or love.

I'll take you away with me somewhere.

Invitation au Voyage

II

Look, how the rain has fallen through the night

and leaves the woods hot, moist and calm,
and the bird skims across the grass
awaiting your return no car in sight.

This is the promised land   a bout du monde

where humid winds play against your calves,

dragon lilies on stone lie open to the sun

and the song of Baudelaire is heard again in afternoon's
     vagabond.

Your eyes are liquid pools where I would drown,

Your lips a history of the heart,

Your hands hot deserts on my back and brow,

and if to die I would do it now,

these words in my mouth

your kiss the vow.

My dear girl, I know in my blood

There is no other way to go on loving you

but this now. Our lives entwined

as an huntsman's bow.

Sunset
(Lieder eines fahrenden gesellen)
to Mahler
Already my spirit soars into the west,

smoke rising from a cigarette

already night's birds begins to fall –

leaves lie quiet on the trees.

Empyrean
Where are you gone —

Lost at the hour of death – and you due

as surely as a bad brand from its flesh –

you were scraped from the womb of your mother
                    cities
          who laughs now and dances in the   canyons
                    of New York City

an ant came and deposited the body of its dead brother
                    on my pillow,

and the very woods in voices of my aunt Ella
                    whispered, Hurt
                    yourself,

hurt yourself in the wind,

                    at three o'clock in the afternoon
without wine.
          incident –
on July 5th I have friends on the East Hampton [illeg]

2.
May 15th – 16 days – May 31
30 days has September and June
                    makes 46
                    plus 5 in July
make 51 days old. The life of a sparrow.

          Edith Piaf.

          I would have named you Peter

     and that day a boy came
was not of the question
he followed me home, 17 yrs old and

and his name was Peter, age 30
when we departed

An organism, Olson calls universe.

"How else can we explain the things that happen to us,
living and breathing." The needs of our
physiological universe"
Yet does it know   [illeg]
when one fraction is lost –
that this blood is boiling inside my brain [. . .]

Magyar –

east of the Urals
your father came
one of
every living one of us
to wreak havoc on Europe, Ugrian people.
even this [illeg] cities of American
speaking no language,

having no poems in your blood.

Only archery, lechery, luxury. I see
the whole press as [illeg]

3.
Yet how can I leave this luxury you offer,
inherited from your grandfather

St. John of the nobler baron race.

New York Steam Co. still owning a few hotels in Cleveland,
    Ohio
Alaska fox furs,   Mahler recordings –   not Mahler
    himself
  as throws for your rug,   that would be too good
    for you,

      twenty dollar cab trips, $95 hosting gowns
[illeg]   – did you know my mother never
    earned $95 a week
no nobility or distinction   in her whole life,
    [illeg]

or the Esterhaus' who kept Hayden on their estate – They
    wouldn't touch you,
non-countess of Hangary, nor even of   as you keep me
         Transylvanian pines
Did they sneak out at night to visit his bedchamber
        by the moon,

     did they see diamonds on his brow,
       or Keep his socks in order.

Before the Storm
The air is heavy with insects,
waiting for rain
clustered under trees.

Your arrival impels me to think

What hurricanes await
What storms ensue

When rain hits these pages,

Trees blow in wind

and lightning strikes the sky.-

All clichés, They say
    but I think of last July
    when rain was tiny footsteps in the wood.
and trees their arms rising to greet them

seeing this
in lightening in the sky,
clouds of heat   massed about the house

        gathered about our ears
each shadow a ghost, each
Wonders what terrors pursue
I had it and lost
(words to write
    on these pages)
in the darkness,   going back
with only cigarettes to see by,

a noose runs over my neck,

footsteps in the grass,

    rustling these pages
each raindrop hits the table top
                  phlop!

Oh ~~God~~ love, have mercy on me
      storm clouds roll   rotate
    as the firefly heads for home

    I head for your arms

    despite the cost of the crash

       of thunder rolls in the sky

       long awaited for,

       now come home

       and rumbling in the kitchen,

       as long before
           too good to hear.

2.

The birds are great and

          gnats
Whimper a little

each man excited in his heart.

Dont go out.

You are an enchanted being.

Even if the world turns inside out

regards you with a sneer,

Seep it as the rain on these pages,

tears of god,
know your fallen condition

your supreme achievement.

          You know

Adversity can be a good thing,

but you have to pay for it the rest of your life.   you know
     everything but deprivation
                              and want,
               which is the greatest gift of them all.
the night stretches sensuously
     practice for the eternal adventure.

          meditation

The Madonna I love,

off the streets and penthouses –

empire buildings over the city,

listening to Bob Dylan

pretending he's real,

When the word is so much more delightful,

eternal and real.

Goodnight, I'm going to bed.
The Furniture Polish Kid

~~Villain or Heroine~~
With You Gone

I saw blood smeared on her eyelids and mouth. woman, what
have you done

what have you done to me?
Are those wounds showing on my hand?

My liver aches so. Have you stamped there, too.

The serpent under foot

I am that snake in the grass,
dishwater in my veins,

The Turned Down Mouth

Approaching thirty-five years of age, for the first time in my life, I experienced leisure, and all that that meant. Time enough to figure out who I was, what I was before this. A film maker, a Bible transliterator, a man on the loose, single, with an endearing passion a desire to be true and firm to the one ~~~~~~~~~~~ of Great Britain now Elizabeth II, Queen of the British Empire, and to the R. H. Philip, Duke of Edinburghe.

I finally discovered my mother, Rose, Ana Luisa y Bourford Fitz of the royal line of Fitz Georges and her late intense son, John F. Kennedy, to be of outbearing heart-rending concern through not so solitary travail in the town to Federal City, where I have spent the last four years, in Buffalo, New York and to uncover the nature of early childhood and penances in Westfrance against my will. Every day I see her as well as her Majesty in my home opposite a small church on a too traveled highway, to town. Despite the mayhems we converse as best we can, observing all and keeping record of the passersby, the impersonators, and the servants, in their regalia and costumes. The police have become a laughing stock, except to these uniformed women officers who guide the school children back and forth to the parochial house.

How distant it seems this evening, how forlorn, how solitary without him whom I truly love, as I love this mother and sister.

I really am brother to Edwarde VIII, HRH, Prince of Wales. Candy shots, I thought of this evening, as a way to distract my enemies from harassing me with cerebral pressures, and to keep peace in Belgian insistence. Underlining rhythm the harmony we seek. All cutheryat all butchery gone. That is for servants. Not for aristocrats, or the purest and twin, whose twin I call myself to beauty.

"Stones bridges under arches."

Why did my brother Edwarde VIII. (Marion, Anne Carnahan,) give up "For the woman I loved," he said. So he must be in love with my wife, Her Royale Highness, Elizabeth II. The Queen of the British Empire, ultimately, who Victoria became, after Vicki's Norfield Shipperd and, I think, Albert C. Niemes, (H. Rider Haggard) is. Louis F. Serbonne write my life story before: Mea culpa and I. P. Semmelweiss, who is on the use of it? I do not give up, for Edwardo Lear still exists through the pen of my sister, et sonamour.

the perspiration between your breasts.

Frogs ache in the night,

       naked under the full moon

I walk, afraid to go in that meadow.

July 3rd

Given to
Rich Kim

The Turned Down Mouth

Approaching thirty-five years of age, for the first time in my life, I experienced leisure, and all that means. Time enough to figure out who I was, what I was before this. A film maker, a Bible transliterator, a man on the loose, single, with one endearing passion, a desire to be true and friend to the one person, who truly loved me; Victoria of Great Britain; now Elizabeth II, Queen to the British Empire, and to the R.H. Philip, Duke of Edinburghe.

I finally discovered my mother, Rose, Ana Luisa of Bourbon, of the royal line of Fitz Georges and her late ~~son~~ interest, John F. Kennedy, to be of ~~endearing~~ heartrending concern through not so solitary travail in the town to Federal City, where I have spent the last four years, in Buffalo, New York. and to uncover the nature of early childhood and penances in New England against my will. Every day I see her as well as her Majesty in my home opposite a small church on a too traveled highway to town. Despite interruptions we converse as best we can, observing all and keeping record of the passersby, the impersonators, and the servants, in their regalia and costumes. The police have become a laughing stock, except for the uniformed women officers who guide the schoolchildren back and forth to the parochial house.

How distant it seems this evening, how forlorn, how solitary, without him whom I truly love, as I love this mother and her late son.

I really am brother to Edward VIII, HRH. Prince of Wales. Candy shoes, I thought of this evening, as a way to distract my enemies from harassing me with cerebral pressure and to keep peace in benign insistence. Underlining rhythm the harmony we seek. All [illeg], all butchery gone. That is for servants. Not for aristocrats, or their parents. And twin, whose twin I call myself to beauty.

"Stoned bridges under arches."

Why did my brother Edward VIII, (Marion, Anne Carnahan) give up the Throne? "For the woman I loved," he said. So he must be in love with my wife, Her Royal Highness, Elizabeth II. The Queen To The British Empire for that "ascended the throne" is ultimately who Victoria became, after Wallis Warfield Simpson and she? said no. I think Albert C. Wieners, (H. Rider Haggard) as Louis F. Destouches wrote my life story before: Mea Culpa and I. P. Semmelweiss, so what's the use of it? I do not give up, for Edward Lear still exists through the pen of my sister, et <u>son amour</u>.

<u>Doll</u>

How many loves had I
in young boy's bed,
at Humarock, or Provincetown's
Cape Cod, under sweating summer sun,

after Land's End, before their interruption.
How many loves had I?

in discourse by firelight, after highballs
to records of Marlene Dietrich and Cole Porter,
how many loves had I?

in Swampscott flat, or Beacon Hill coachhouse,
Beacon Street garage or Fiedler overpass,
how many loves had I?

How many loves, in Annandale,
before payment or threat, in the Public Gardens
or Fifth Avenue park, how many loves –

None, none, none at all.

En Famille

When a young man after graduation from the University of Boston College, I moved in town to the city of Boston to live on Beacon Hill and fulfill the role of artist I had chosen while an undergraduate in the year 1950 at the age of sixteen as a freshman in my fifth year of study with the Society of Jesus.

How anxious I was to attend the University! How full of excitement, how innocent of the world and its wiles, and grateful to Father — Morrisey for a letter of introduction to the Director of the Libraries for a scholarship to provide for my tuition of $450 a year. I had to pay for my books, my transportation and clothing, though my patient and hard-working Mother and her family would graciously load me with presents and funds at Christmas and birthday. Nevertheless I had to work twenty hours a week, the school year, and five and a half days a week during the summer months at the salary of $27.50 per week. I could not stand this more than one summer and at the end of the second year I quit, due to tardiness, and was employed at the Jordan Marsh Co. at the salary of $35.00 per week for forty hours work. I was working forty six hours a week at the Bapst Memorial library under Terence F. Connoly and in the summer took one hour and a half by expensive trolley and undercurrent train to arrive at Chestnut Hill for exciting and varied employment in the Catalog Room and the stacks, occasionally to replace someone at Lunch Hour in the Main Reading Room at the Circulation Desk or to slice leaves of imported French journals and check coats on the first floor outside the auditorium; then another hour and a half return to home, and my loving family of Father, he too returned from 14 hours a day employment in a series of office buildings throughout the city; Mother, Sister, and two brothers of unique charm and extraordinary talent, still possessing both to the present day of 1969.

A Rose in the Devil's Garden

Edith

I never entered springtime
everytime you do you lose
we stayed together all summer long
how she tortured me

Is that why you look funny
walk mincingly with one eye
my little butterfly, John look

here's another one. they took my tear ducts away

from the Duke of Albany   1969

my own little book
then we became ministers in Berlin and
loved no one with no initials
he threw me out a window
of a boarding house
on Geary Street.

Pest

I live in a flop
half-looped,
blood stains on skirt
nor chained to a bed,

a phantom kiss for company
communicating archly
by Anne the terror of
tenement tragedy.

Passers-by perhaps
recognize the face
to promenade in
chance their glance

populates disbarred midnight

A Family Strain

Paul Verlaine created a condition of treachery in Rome
by using roots of the mandrake tree to sterilize himself and
then run amok on the street, castrated, one of the slaves that
Imperial Caesar used to punish as a hypocrite, for betrayal of
marriage vows.

Adulterous Verlaine still succours himself with onions;
son and bacon fat, two close relations to this party. One he

places in seedy legal transaction and the other in government treason, arts he learned himself in bedlam, by North African niggers; travelling, shooting mercenaries, heads swollen by the sun to anger and impatience, faults he inflicts upon naivete through obsession, sucession and repression.

So long he has dwelt upon the bawd, his load collapsed, Hapsburg wastes of swamp and pestilential fever, buzzing droves.

Saracen riot blades cut him down, Scythian scythes drove him mad, how much more could his attention take. A family strain to slake. Unfortunately he was not needed, until he declared himself neighbor and began lisping as a woman outside my office, something no one in my family has ever done. Thus I doubt he may displace us, or impose his practices in the United States, as he did in London and Constantinople, where he was born in a whorehouse, among merchants. They named it Indo-China and they still fight there in the jungle rot.

Swish

Exposed
two misleads
more penetratingly than I

not willing to admit it
put out
at least you have someone to go to

relatively new to earth.
of course we can remember these things
in our sleep.

aching dryness
horrible hunger
a parched loneliness

artly compensation

Misunderstaning
O Beaulah lonely one
more fraud on Edward Taylor son

you've gone blind from overwork
You mean you don't know what day it is.
I'm a day behind myself

Of giving money to people of that
I'm not guilty
I'm not that guilty

immigrants allowed to ask questions

I won't leave my own shop
I do my own shopping.

        My family

     were for the most part, thieves, following the example of
Henry, Duke of Gloucester.
     My mother was fat, toothless and coarse.
     My father was bald, toothless and mute.

My sister was mad, from a need for superiority.
My brothers were bald, toothless and hebretonic.

They stank literally in their obsession with material goods, in their indulgence for speed, blindness and danger, relentlessly hunting in various disguises for punishment to anything they saw, following me from city to city, occupation to education for satisfaction of their depleted appetites, based on alcohol, poison, and abuse of the human person, leading themselves to degradation and anyone who knew them.

Their habits were brusque and non-productive, resisting anyone who disapproved of their methods of cannibalism, and wantonness. I have heard and seen them brawl until late in the evening over beer and cards, in disgusting indulgence of the most vulgar sort, until they were halted by bayonet and explosion of their terrible practices.

I left them when I was at the age of twenty years.
They have followed me ever since, tearing apart my skull, digesting the marrow of my bones, scarring the epidermis and burning their hideous flesh, flapping off rancid bones.

Their names are Albert Eugene Wieners. He lives under the pseudonyms of Robert White Creeley, Albert Eugene Wieners, Junior, Robert Barrett Wieners; he calls himself my father.

She lives under the names of Anna Elizabeth Laffan Wieners. She calls herself my mother. She is 68 years of age and under the care of her daughter, who poses as a <u>physician</u> on Brush Hill Road in the town of Milton in the state of Massachusetts. She also smells under the name of <u>Eleanor</u> "Forbes," possibly a non-entity. the name of Ann Laughlin and for hours, she ingests every known poison and commits herself to lowering my mentality, a condition that so infuriates me I usually write to the <u>Attorney General's</u> Office in Federal City, District of Columbia, or to the <u>Chief of Police</u> in their small town by the banks of the Neponset River in the State of Massachusetts, or to the <u>District Attorney</u> in same state, to which they emigrated from the outcast huts of the Kingdom of Ireland.

Her accomplice has always been the reptile.

When I go to the hospital, they are there.

At the library, they are absent or are the form of respectable people, or in an earlier stage, of unknowing, or devotion. I do not mind them then.

Now with the aid of their eldest daughter, Marion Fances Wieners Malinowski, who lives under owned property in the names of Anne Mullaney Laffan at 665 East Eighth Street in the city of South Boston in the state of Massachusetts.

Fashion Design
Introduced by
Donald Wieners as Master of Ceremonies

Mary   Silhouette=   ivory <u>satin</u> double skirt
                    bow at thorax
skin supports   bow on either hip – mid thigh
    2 escorts   bow
Edward Binky Albert Wieners   <u>black</u> satin sheath with
        thorax extending through costume,
              and through hip places. Hip bows of <u>velvet</u> rope
              2 bows at knees optional.
              starched tiara of ivory lace. Rainproof lace and
    wig.
    <u>Nostalgia</u>
Marion Frances   1 Blue Strapless <u>tulle</u> full length evening
        costume
                2 Blue cape frosting: diamond coat of family
    arms stitched on backs.
no underwear alone   3 Lemon lining to cape, natural
    lemon leg wear of <u>silk</u>
<u>no low</u> décolleté   4 Topaz ring. Hazel coiffure
freckled thorax   5 white arm length gloves of linen

    <u>Snow White</u>
Christina   2 diamond 2 foot hoops upholding
                white <u>cotton</u> ball <u>dress</u>, black patent leather
nylon   sandals, diamond buckles. White
        cotton full length
handwoven   stockings, diamond ring, <u>black</u> bangs,
        black ear lobe
    <u>Prince Charming</u>   <u>Dutch Bob</u>. natural manicure, bare
    arms, no cloak
        Richard Cummings   diamond back clasp.
                diamond girdle.

207

Belle　　　　　　Fabric Brocade
Anna　　　　　　　　Dress optional: but open at delta over
lace underclothing　　　　tea rose pendant
　　Designer
　　John Wieners　　　Fur neckpiece of white rabbit optional
　　　　　　gift box, white live bunny
　　　　　　Flowered crown of circlet open buds

　　Violets
　　　　　　Panel of violets as train
Johan M Dockoff　　　With preserved shrunken kernels along
　　　bodice of wheat
　　　　　　White wheat empire formal
　　　　　　White wheat empire pumps
　　alone　　　　Empire clasp
　　　　　White leotards　　　of wheat.
$50 each model
$50 each escort & master of ceremonies.
　　　　　　lost $500

　black satin calf jodphurs

　　Pastille

No matter how loaded you get him
he will always come home,
though I am not his only home

in my reverie
he gave you a swift kick
on the street this morning,

mistress or wife
you are not my only home,
refuge, or hole,

with windows too low
for spiritual bastille
outside our door.

Degospelson

All kinds of speculation here in my brain as to the ancestry
of the proprietor of a bookshop on Allen Street in Buffalo, this
evening, who I suspect from my visions may be a Holy German
Emperor as well as my father, the man who raised me under
the name of John, when my mother, the woman, who raised
me, preferred to have me called Edward, after the doctor, or
one of them who bore me into this world. The other's name
was Harvey, their last names Greenblatt and Moynihan.

I am the Holy German Emperor Frederick III and am
threatened by a cruel bald named Albert Eugene Wieners,
Junior of 89 Hawthorne Road, Braintree, Massachusetts.
He practices (medicine) under the name of Helena Murphy,
gynecologist on Brush Hill Road, Milton, Massachusetts and
he had me illegally committed to two hospitals and a sanitarium
in Massachusetts, where I was <u>cannibalized</u> and electrocuted,
having become victim to their excesses of hysteria, sodomy, and
castration. How I despise this last named person, who practices

still horrors upon human infants and women, torturing them with drugs and confinement for excitement and slavery.

He writes under and profits from the names of William Manchester and Allen Drury, and uses <u>me</u> as his favorite guinea pig.

The proprietor of this bookshop has saved me thousands of situations where I was compromised, a victim of ignominy, revenge, and indulgence, practiced by his liege, or lieutenant, a poet and biographer, Paul Joseph.

The proprietor's name as I believe is Serge Eisen, my name was once Sergei Y Essene – We have been photographed together by L. Eisen.

Frederick Heinrich Eberstatdt Yessenin

Rimbaud Fraud

Demuth   Leger

Courbet   Manet

Possibly, the torment of beauty obsesses the drugged viewer, pining and avenging bottom forlornly repenting the horror of condition.

The tenement slave writhing this moment in prison of ridicule and disgrace infects all men by cowardness and blindness, impersonating health, intelligence and labor with attaching herself to same, when truth fully he continues to poison men who despise and condemn his every move.

Painted as the Belgian Nude, I was beset with this idiot companion. Her name Marion Frances Wieners now become Mrs John Malinowski, Junior, a <u>friend</u> at home, in the city and worse alone incompetent to partake of either. Best to commit this victim to a work farm, where she serves as an example of failure to manage her affairs honestly.

She needs chemicals of reptiles and rodents to survive. She knows sewers and exclusion from friendship and in seeing paintings, hearing music, watching the dance, composing poetry, she may only feel chagrin, poverty, and pantomime.

Her need to destroy the creators of these forms renders her a menace to them.

She claims to be a sister of Jeane Arthur, a person whom she knew from childhood, who no longer cares for her company, since or as she will not purify her attention.

That consists of repetition, vacancy, false feeling and reported observation to threaten innocence, distance and historical memory.

Crippled motivation the uppermost agent informs her occupation one wishes removed from conduct of society, an activity harmed through her presence, already traced during the predominance of hospitals, rude restaurants and uncivil manners present in force.

Positioning vulgarly in small towns on prominent location, sickening the meeting places, the books and young men, their futures narrowed at such principles. The individual actually reacts without reason towards an object, seizing upon it as an escape, seeing in control a vituperative and constrained bigot, despot or dictator.

Couple this with an already artistic parent, completely at home with a higher example of interest in these same outlets as painting, poetry, politics and public prominence, the ability to function without insult diminishes

Thus the true creator ceases to be alone and continues to hear rejoicing and exultation in a loved one, without onerous slugs of self-protection.

We expect to be protected by these tenement slaves, minus loud months in parking lots or brash orders in commerce as I am most guilty of, in dining out, of commanding paid servitors from in opportune training received with deprived progenitors.

Gratefully, we welcome their compliance as audience, partner and aid.

To exist side by side with an artist is easy, if he is successful, and all of them are, despite suicide, or disappearance, exhibition and postured role.

One must accept that place, the person definitely cultivated valuably as one self, desirously a great talent to be shared in his beholders.

age 34 years

Stars Seen in Person

1963 –
1969   Virginia Mayo   The Student Bookshop
       and daughter   Buffalo, New York

       Larry Parks   The University Delicatessen
       & party of three   Buffalo, New York

Buster Crabbe   "   "   "
Jane Withers

William "Buck" Rodgers   The Harvey Restaurant
and female companion &   San Francisco
young man   California

Janet Blair   The Blue Galaxie

Amy Vanderbilt   The Hot Dog House
company of secretary w/lunch

Lily Palmer with   The Player
 girl friend   shopping

Lewis Stone with   Onetta's
   date dining

Eddie Albert   West 57th Street
strolling after Health Club   New York

George Raft   Buffalo   New
driving Main Street

Mickey Rooney   "   York

Lana Turner   The Park Lane
        together at   Gates Circle
Joan Bennett Sunday brunch   New York

Lucille Ball   Loew's Teck
Saturday Matinee of the Star   Buffalo New York
Marilyn Monroe   Bus Station
Katharine Cornell

Zsa Zsa Gabor

[drawing – see facsimile p.19 of orig journal]

Joan Fontaine   Radio City Music Hall
alone in crowd at matinee break   April 1969

Jeanette MacDonald
alone
Rita Hayworth   The George Washington Hotel
alone   Revolving- April 1969

Steve Cochrane   Main Street
with a plainclothesman

Dana Andrews   1963 8th Street
with bodyguards   New York

John Barrymore, Junior   1965 Four Corners
alone   Los Angeles

Hamilton Fancher III   1965 California
alone in

Anne Baxter   Century Theater
alone

Warner Baxter &
wife

Penn Central Train
to New York City

Jane Fonda with
mom
Gloria Grahame
in Hansom Cab

at Rumplemeyer's
St. Moritz Hotel
Central Park South

Henry Morgan
strolling Central Park

1966

Rose Kennedy with
companion

Hengerer's
New York

Carol Channing working
alone & with date at
SUNYAB

1969

Greta Garbo
as waitress & supper date
after antiquing

Onetta's
1969

Marlene Dietrich backseat
driven in car with three

Joan Leslie

Jane Greer

Viveca Lindfors returning from
The Colonial to the Ritz Carlton

1955

Hermione Gringold outside
Schubert Theatre Boston

1957

Vincent Price on way to appearance Pilgrim Theatre, Boston
1956

Robert Ryan
in elevator at the Dakota   1966
Hotel

Robert Cummings in front of Newman Club

Tony Curtis at Renato's
with date

Jacqueline Onassis

Merv Griffin

Johnnie Carson
outside St. Patrick's Cathedral   1954

Burgess Meredith backstage   1968
at the
with young society model

Juan Paul Belmondo
with Coccinelle

Fernadel

Bobby Driscoll   Epiphany   Hotel Nassau
          New York   1967

Dean Stockwell   The Gov. Douglas Ranch
                    Tucson, Arizona 1965
Morey Amsterdam

Robert Taylor night
Saturday shopping

Theodore Rothschild

Maggie Paley – Mrs

Vera Lorina   1968

Priscilla Morgane   Rome, Italy
William Morris Agency   Allegro Nationale 1966

Fred Astaire
strolling in good humor   1969

Rosalind Russell   New York 1955
   alone up Fifth Avenue
   to Hotel Pierre

Jane Powell

Diana Lynn

[illeg] St. Martin

[illeg] von Allenbergh
at the Plaza with table of
two

Jean Peters working
at the University

Dyan Cannon entering
Lee's Drugstore alone

Peter Lorre outside upper
   Times Square Theatre

Ida Lupino   1960
  Times Square

Ethel Merman
Idelwild Sunday evening

Suzy Parker led by date

Dorothy Lamour with
May Thompson
in Max's Kansas City

Cholly Knickerbocker

Claire Trevor
crossing Lower Broadway

George Sanders
passing in Cadillac

Rip Torn

Geraldine Page at home

Ingrid Bergman
with two ladies outside
Walgreen's

Hedy Lemarr
with children on expressway

Sol Spiegel

Peggy Lee and husband

The power Flowers
in memoriam to Victoria-Eugenie

On a squalid back porch
during a storm of dust
I read my death notice

in yesterday's newspaper,
granddaughter to Queen Victoria
born in Balmoral Castle,

the first nativity
since my mother Mary
in the fifteenth century.

Who am I to wonder
before the thunder and
the squall, the encircling burden

of parenthood, fraternity
and equality encompassing
my attitude toward this state

I have chosen,
as haven for memory's spirit,
an alienated homestead.

The sun finally emerged
in the center of a field
toward blue clouds waved,

a burst of reward,
unearned by thieves
in possession of these bones.

How lovely with them gorged
in the corrupt bodies of traitors
and servitors, irresponsible

for conception, unremiss
of upbringing, hoarding
frailty's hours.

LOST & FOUND: The CUNY Poetics Document Initiative publishes primary sources by figures associated with New American Poetry in an annual series of chapbooks under the general editorship of Ammiel Alcalay. *Lost & Found's* aim is to open the field of inquiry and illuminate the terrain of an essential chapter of twentieth-century letters. The series has published little-known work by Kathy Acker, Amiri Baraka, Diane di Prima, Robert Duncan, Langston Hughes, Frank O'Hara, Margaret Randall, Muriel Rukeyser, and many others.

Under the auspices of The Center for the Humanities, and with the guidance of an extended scholarly community, *Lost & Found* chapbooks are researched and prepared by students and guest fellows at the PhD Program in English of the Graduate Center of the City University of New York. Utilizing personal and institutional archives, *Lost & Found* scholars seek to broaden our literary, cultural, and political history.

LOST & FOUND ELSEWHERE is a unique new series of book-length projects emerging from the research of *Lost & Found* editors. Working in partnership with select publishers, these books bring to light unpublished or long unavailable materials that have emerged alongside or as part of the *Lost & Found* project. Available in this series:

Robert Duncan in San Francisco	*A Walker in the City: Elegy for Gloucester*	*Savage Coast*	*Amiri Baraka and Edward Dorn: The Collected Letters*
Michael Rumaker	Peter Anastas	Muriel Rukeyser	
Expanded edition edited by Ammiel Alcalay and Megan Paslawski	With an afterword by Ammiel Alcalay	Edited with an introduction by Rowena Kennedy-Epstein	Edited by Claudia Moreno Pisano
CITY LIGHTS PUBLISHERS	BACK SHORE PRESS	THE FEMINIST PRESS	UNIVERSITY OF NEW MEXICO PRESS
			Winner of the 2014 Pen Oakland Josephine Miles Award

For more information, visit lostandfoundbooks.org